The Nyasaland
Elections of 1961

by
LUCY MAIR
*Reader in Applied Anthropology
in the London School of Economics*

UNIVERSITY OF LONDON
Published for the
Institute of Commonwealth Studies
THE ATHLONE PRESS
1962

Published by
THE ATHLONE PRESS
UNIVERSITY OF LONDON
at 2 Gower Street, London WC1
Distributed by Constable & Co Ltd
12 *Orange Street, London* WC2
Canada
University of Toronto Press
Toronto, 5
U.S.A.
Oxford University Press Inc
New York

Printed in Great Britain by
WESTERN PRINTING SERVICES LTD
BRISTOL

NOTE

This study was made possible by a grant from the Colonial Social Science Research Council. Like all studies financed in this way, it had no official character and was not in any sense an enquiry on behalf of, or a report to, a government. I am solely responsible for every statement made in it.

I should like to record my thanks to the Supervisor of Elections and the Nyasaland Information Department for their kindness in answering questions and their help in enabling me to visit polling and registration stations and follow the work of information teams; to the headquarters officials of all the parties; and to those candidates who allowed me to follow in detail the progress of their campaigns.

September 1961

L.M.

THE NYASALAND ELECTIONS OF 1961

1. Organization

THE CONSTITUTIONAL BACKGROUND

The elections of 1961 were not the first ever to be held for the Nyasaland Legislative Council, since the European members of that body had been directly elected in 1956. The method of selection of non-official members of the Council had evolved along the lines generally characteristic of British dependencies. From 1907 six non-officials were nominated by the Governor, one of them being charged with the representation of African interests;[1] as elsewhere, it was the convention to choose a missionary for the latter purpose.

Shortly before the second world war a number of bodies representative of non-African interest-groups combined to form a Convention of Associations, which met about five times a year and agreed on communications to Government on matters raised by its members. This and the Chamber of Commerce were regarded as the appropriate bodies to submit names to the Governor for nomination. The two organizations did not always co-operate, though leading personalities in the Convention of Associations were members of the Chamber of Commerce.

The two bodies in 1945 submitted proposals for constitutional change. The Convention of Associations envisaged a council of twenty-two members in addition to the Governor. Of these, twelve would have been non-officials, four representing Europeans, two Asians, one 'Anglo-African' and three Africans, with two (who would in practice have been Europeans) nominated to represent agriculture and commerce respectively. The four representative Europeans were to be directly elected; of those representing other communities all but one were to be nominated from panels submitted by appropriate bodies, a procedure which does not seem, in the case of the Convention of Associations, to have resulted in any interference with the nominating body's first choice. The appropriate associations for Asians and Anglo-Africans would be those already formed to represent their interests. For the Africans one name should come from each of two newly constituted bodies: the Provincial Councils and the Nyasaland African Congress. The former consisted of a majority of Native Authorities selected from among the membership of District Councils of Chiefs, with a minority

[1] Nyasaland Order in Council, S.R.O. 541, 1907, and Royal Instructions, 9 August 1907.

of non-chiefs appointed on their recommendation; the latter was a voluntary body consisting of educated Africans, mostly at that time in government service. The third African should be appointed by the Governor.

The Chamber of Commerce was only interested in the representation of Europeans, and asked for direct elections.

After considering these proposals the Government produced a modified version, in which the balance within the twenty-two members was different. These were to be nominated, not necessarily as representatives of special interests. There would be nine officials and ten non-officials, five European, two Asian and three African. None of these would be directly elected. Three Europeans would be selected by the Convention of Associations, one by the Northern Province Association (a member of the Convention) and one by the Chamber of Commerce. The Asians would be selected by 'suitable bodies' and all the Africans by the Protectorate Council which had now been set up to represent the three Provincial Councils.

The President of the Convention of Associations, however, argued that the differences between this plan and the Convention's proposals were not significant, and commended it to the members' consideration in a speech which emphasized, in terms of general benevolence, the importance of inter-racial co-operation. 'This country is only at the beginning of its political life and we have all to learn by co-operation and real endeavour to try to understand the problems of our many races and peoples and how best the country can be administered for the greatest good and benefit of all of us.'

The upshot of confidential discussions appears to have been, however, that the European community as a whole regarded a constitution of the type proposed as premature.

The changes which in fact became effective in 1949 were described by the then Secretary of State as a step in the direction of representative government. However, they amounted to no more than the addition to the existing number of non-officials of two Africans and an Asian, and of three more official members to balance them. The African members were to be selected by the Governor from names put forward by the Protectorate Council, the Asian from names put forward by the Indian Chamber of Commerce. No further changes were made until 1956.[1]

In that year elections, direct for non-Africans and indirect for Africans, were introduced for the first time. The qualifications for the non-African franchise were literacy and an income of £200 or property worth £250. Six members were elected on this franchise. Five Africans were chosen by the Provincial Councils, a total electorate of seventy-

[1] Legislative Council Ordinance 25 of 1955.

six. The legislature constituted by these elections remained in existence till 1961, its life having been extended for a year on account of the state of emergency which was in force from March 1959 to May 1960.

There had, however, been discussion of the next phase of constitutional advance. A delegation from the Nyasaland African Congress in 1957 placed before the Governor a plan for a legislature of forty members elected by universal suffrage and an executive council elected by it. In discussion they agreed to compromise to the extent of allowing eight seats in the legislature for non-Africans and two in the executive council for officials. The Governor indicated that he would consult with the non-African communities and put forward alternative proposals. No such proposals had been formulated by June 1958, when a delegation to London, this time headed by Dr. Hastings Kamuzu Banda, put the original African plan before the Secretary of State (Mr. Lennox-Boyd). The latter replied that the Governor's recommendations were expected shortly. Some further discussion was held with Dr. Banda after his return to Nyasaland, but the declaration of the emergency put an end to negotiations, which were not resumed until the Secretary of State (Mr. Iain Macleod) met Dr. Banda in May 1960.

As soon as the emergency was declared at an end arrangements were made for further constitutional discussions, and these were held at Lancaster House in July. All sections of opinion held to be significant were represented. The conditions of Nyasaland at that time being what they were, these were not reducible to tidy categories. The United Federal Party could be identified reasonably enough with general European opinion, but its delegation included, in addition to Messrs. Dixon, Blackwood and Little, Members of Legislative Council, Mr. Mathews Phiri, who had been a leading Congress member but joined the U.F.P. on his release from detention a few weeks after the declaration of the emergency. The constitutionally recognized representatives of African opinion were Mr. Chinyama and Mr. Kwenje, two of the three African M.L.C's who had dissociated themselves from Dr. Banda and retained their seats during the emergency. For the Malawi Congress Party, Dr. Banda brought with him Mr. Orton Chirwa, Mr. W. K. Chiume (who had been an M.L.C., but whose seat had been declared vacant when the Nyasaland African Congress was banned) and Mr. Aleke Banda, his personal secretary. The Congress Liberation Party was represented by Mr. T. D. T. Banda, and the Asian Association by Mr. Sattar Sacranie. In accordance with the view that the most appropriate spokesmen of the rural Africans are still their chiefs, five were chosen to represent them by the whole body of Native Authorities.

The proceedings of the conference were not made public, but obviously the question of the franchise was its most controversial point.

The opposing views could easily have been predicted. Dr. Banda, like all other African leaders in such circumstances, pressed for 'one man, one vote', while the U.F.P., following its principle of advancement by 'merit not race', sought to ensure that the franchise should be limited to 'responsible' persons. In the complex set of alternative qualifications which were eventually accepted a number of criteria were used. None of these were new; but one might question whether any one of them is in fact a guarantee of sound political judgment, in itself a highly subjective concept. Their practical effect was to limit the numbers of the electorate. As the number of seats was fixed in advance, a larger electorate could not mean a larger number of African voices in the legislature.

The Secretary of State described the task of the conference as being 'to seek a pattern for the orderly evolution of Nyasaland's political institutions on a democratic basis, in a form which would meet the aspirations and apprehensions of the peoples of Nyasaland'. The principle accepted with regard to African representation was that it 'should be obtained by direct elections, based on a reasonable and broad franchise suited to the present conditions of the country'.

THE LANCASTER HOUSE AGREEMENT

The agreement that was reached[1] produced what must be the most complicated franchise to have been devised even in Central Africa; though the task of registering authorities was simplified in the event by the fact that the majority of those applying for registration offered the same qualifications.

Nyasaland was to be divided into twenty-eight constituencies, in twenty of which representatives should be elected on a lower and in eight on a higher franchise. The Executive Council was to include five officials, three ex-officio and two nominated, two members elected on the higher and three on the lower roll. The five official members of the Executive Council were to be members of the legislature. The Executive Council was still to be advisory to the Governor.

All voters were required to be over twenty-one years old, to have been resident in the Protectorate for two years at any time prior to registration, and to be either British subjects or 'British protected persons belonging to Nyasaland'. The qualifications for the higher franchise were identical with those for ordinary voters in Northern Rhodesia.

Applicants to qualify on the lower roll could satisfy various alternatives, which combined in different proportions education, income and evidence of 'responsibility'. Persons who were literate in English

---

[1] *Report of the Nyasaland Constitutional Conference*, Cmnd. 1132, 1960.

and had an income of over £120 or property worth £250 were qualified if they had reached the minimum age of twenty-one, whereas all others had to be older. This was not explicitly stated, but was the consequence of the explicit requirements. Of these the one which the majority of those registering were able to satisfy was that they should be literate in any language in common use in the country and have paid tax (or have been exempt from payment) for ten years. The primary object of this provision was not, as might appear, to ensure that voters had met their financial obligations, but to establish a minimum age. The U.F.P. had sought to fix the age of political discretion at forty years, but it was found that the necessary tax records were not available. The ten-year requirement was agreed to on the understanding that all districts had records for this period. Since liability for tax begins at eighteen, this gives a minimum age of twenty-seven or twenty-eight, and was cal-culated to exclude a number of the more militant supporters of Malawi. Persons occupying certain social statuses were held to be *prima facie* 'responsible' even if not literate. These were chiefs and headmen, mem-bers of Native Authorities and past or present members of district councils, Master Farmers (i.e. men adjudged by the Agricultural De-partment to have attained certain standards), pensioners (i.e. persons retired from pensionable employment—there are, of course, no old-age pensioners) and ex-servicemen.

To Dr. Banda the principle 'one man, one vote' has always implied the enfranchisement of women. The general feeling of the conference appears to have been opposed to this, and it can certainly be argued that in such a country as Nyasaland few women are equal to their brothers in awareness of political issues. The point was made—it is said by Mr. Sacranie, the president of the Asian Association—that there were some highly educated women who could not reasonably be refused the vote. Women graduates are said to have been mentioned; there were believed to be one or two in Nyasaland. The conference agreed in principle that a woman should be entitled to qualify either in her own right or in vir-tue of her husband's qualifications, but left the detailed provisions on this point to be settled by the Working Party which would be respon-sible for implementing its general recommendations. The U.F.P. stated later that they agreed on the understanding that only women who had professional qualifications would be enfranchised; this could cer-tainly not be deduced from the wording of the White Paper.

It was estimated at the time of the agreement that about 100,000 Africans would qualify for the vote. Calculations based on numbers of children in school were held to make it probable that the number of literates was much larger. Malawi triumphantly asserted that Dr. Banda had secured 'one man, one vote, by the back door', so confident were they of the ease with which the qualifications could be met. It was also widely believed that Dr. Banda had secured the vote for all women. In the months between the agreement and the opening of registration the figure of 200,000 was sometimes mentioned, and occasionally 250,000, though official arrangements were based throughout on the assumption that 100,000 voters should be registered. The United Federal Party related these higher estimates to modifications in the registration provisions which, according to them, departed from the principles agreed on at Lancaster House.

The qualifications for the higher roll were more complicated than those which had been required for the non-African electorate in 1956, and rather more restrictive. In 1956 non-African voters were required to 'have an adequate knowledge of the English language' and have an income of £200 or property worth £250. Under the new legislation university graduates were not required to have any further qualification, but for others the lowest requirement was an income of £300 or property of £500 combined with secondary education. With income of £480 or property worth £1,000, primary education was sufficient to qualify, while persons with an income of £720 or property worth £1,500 were not required to show any educational qualification at all beyond the ability to complete a registration form in English.

THE WORKING PARTY'S REPORT

The Working Party provided for in the Lancaster House agreement consisted of the Attorney General, Mr. J. B. Pine, and the Director of Local Government, Mr. C. Winnington-Ingram. In addition to making a study of electoral organization in other emergent states, it held discussions and received memoranda from representatives of all the groups which took part in the London conference 'with a view to meeting their representations so far as seemed to us proper and possible within our terms of reference'. The U.F.P. maintained that this was not enough, and that they should have received something in the nature of periodic progress reports enabling them to object to what they considered to be departures from the agreement. The report[1] was completed and signed on 15 October and submitted to the Secretary of State, who approved it with a number of amendments.

The report stated that the Working Party had been guided by two principles. The first was simplicity. This word rang rather hollow in the ears of the officials who were charged with such tasks as explaining the electoral qualifications and preparing the different types of form to be filled in by applicants offering different qualifications. Nevertheless,

[1] *Report of the Constitutional Working Party*, Nyasaland Protectorate, 1961.

given the complicated rules which had been agreed upon at Lancaster House, the Working Party did its best not to introduce additional complications. The second principle was the desirability of choosing the definition which enfranchises the most people when more than one definition satisfies the criterion of simplicity. In one respect the Working Party's report expressly differed from what was agreed to at Lancaster House. This concerned the fundamental nationality qualification. The original requirement was that voters must be British subjects or British Protected Persons 'belonging to Nyasaland'. A person is defined as a British Protected Person if he was born in a protectorate or if his father was born in a protectorate.[1] A peculiar feature of Nyasaland is the steady immigration into the territory of Africans from Portuguese East Africa. Some are simply seeking employment, others are rejoining tribal groups from which the frontier divides them. It is not practically possible to distinguish them from those who were, or whose fathers were, born in the country, since records of births are not kept. The Working Party argued that such people do in fact 'belong to Nyasaland'. It is their home, they are in no way distinguishable from the communities among which they live and they are registered as taxpayers. This is also true of a smaller number of people who are British Protected Persons because they or their fathers were born in Northern Rhodesia or Tanganyika. Arguing that all such persons would be entitled to qualify for a vote by obtaining British nationality but that it would be unreasonable to require this of them, the Working Party decided to follow the distinction made for taxation purposes between 'Nyasaland Africans' and 'immigrant Africans' and to admit to registration anyone who was included in the former category.

This decision was regarded by the U.F.P. as a breach of the Lancaster House agreement, and indeed it bulked large enough in their list of grievances against British policy for Sir Roy Welensky to mention it when he addressed the Conservative members of Parliament in March 1961.[2] I did not hear any U.F.P. representative maintain that the change would be likely materially to affect the course of the elections. Their protests took the form that no agreement should be changed without the consent of all parties and that it is in principle wrong to enfranchise people whose allegiance is to another government. Some of them, however, maintained that justice now called for the enfranchisement of European Portuguese living in Nyasaland.

It had been left to the Working Party to determine the conditions on which women should vote. The various suggestions made to it doubt-

[1] British Protectorates, Protected States or Protected Persons Order in Council, 1949. S. I., 1949, No. 140.
[2] Reported in *The Times*, 18 March 1961.

less repeat proposals made at Lancaster house—that the franchise should be extended to all wives of qualified voters, to literate women over twenty-one, and to literate women who had attained the stage of 'respectable motherhood' (this last was Dr. Banda's phrase). The criterion actually imposed was in effect an age qualification roughly corresponding to that required of men who could not meet the property qualification. Such men had to have paid tax for ten years and so would be at least twenty-eight years old. The requirement for women (along with literacy, as for men) was that they should have been married for ten years, though not necessarily to the same husband throughout the period. Since a good many women probably marry before they are eighteen, this made the qualifying age rather lower for women.

This too was regarded by the U.F.P. as a breach of faith. A U.F.P. organizer said indignantly that now a woman could vote if she had had ten husbands in ten years. This suggests a rather different criterion of political responsibility from any that had been discussed at Lancaster House, and invites one to speculate on the relative political acumen of, say, Mme. du Chastelet and the average Women's Institute member. Women could, of course, legally qualify on the basis of income and as holders of some of the 'scheduled posts'. There were one or two women Native Authorities, for example. They could also qualify in virtue of their husband's income, if they were themselves literate, and a number did so.

The argument originally put forward at Lancaster House, that women graduates should be entitled to vote irrespective of other qualifications, was extended by the Working Party to the proposition that all graduates should be qualified *ipso facto* and should be entitled to register on either the higher or lower roll, an arrangement which may reflect the belief that Africans would prefer to vote on the roll on which they were the majority, or may have been connected with the provision (later amended) that candidates must be registered on the same roll as those whose votes they were seeking.

When the Working Party came to look into the state of the tax registers, they found that in a good many districts these did not go back for more than six years. In these places, they concluded, the registration officers would have to judge from an applicant's appearance whether he was of the required age. (The application forms of course included the question whether the applicant had paid tax for ten years and the usual warning that it was an offence to make a false declaration.)

To this change also the U.F.P. objected. At the conference, they asserted, they agreed to abandon their demand for a minimum age of 40 only when they were assured that tax records for the past ten years were everywhere available, and it is true that the arrangement adopted left a good deal of room for error; it might be easier to judge whether an African looked old enough to have paid tax for five years than whether he looked old enough to have paid for ten. It would be going too far to say that the qualifying age is now nearer 25 than 30, but this was the U.F.P. interpretation. They did not say how the situation should have been dealt with, but implied that they would have maintained their demand for a voting age of 40 and could have obtained this. But even a minimum of 25 excluded many of the Malawi Youth (if this was the aim of the U.F.P. and the intention of Mr. Macleod).

Sir Roy Welensky at the U.F.P. general conference in Salisbury in February 1961 demanded an investigation by the British Government—into the conduct of the Working Party, presumably. In the main one has to infer the logical grounds of their dissatisfaction. Their declared policy was that government—and therefore the choice of a government—should be in the hands of 'responsible' persons, but the implication of their attitude seems to be that the smaller the electorate for whatever reason, the more responsible it must be.

The nature of their electoral calculations can be deduced from a statement made officially not by them but by the chairman at a protest meeting of the Settlers' and Residents' Association, a body which from time to time passed resolutions pledging support to Sir Roy Welensky but described itself as non-political. According to him it was the deliberate intention of the Secretary of State by 'debasing the lower roll franchise' to secure Malawi representation in the twenty lower-roll constituencies and so be able to discount 'the importance of moderate views'.[1] In other words, the admittedly small number of U.F.P. supporters would carry more weight in a smaller total electorate. No serious attempt was made to show that the criteria adopted by the Working Party admitted to the franchise classes of person qualitatively inferior to those specified at Lancaster House.

The Working Party came down squarely in favour of voluntary registration. A completely automatic registration would not have been practicable with a franchise of the type they were dealing with, though there are records of a few of the persons holding 'scheduled posts'—chiefs, members of District Council and Master Farmers; village headmen are apparently not easily identifiable by the authorities.

They rejected the suggestion that those who were registered for the non-African franchise in 1956 should be automatically re-registered, on the ground that the qualifications required then did not correspond to those for either the higher or the lower roll. The U.F.P., however, obtained from the Secretary of State an amendment providing that 'any person who fails to qualify under the new franchise but who is registered

[1] *Nyasaland Times*, 28 February 1961.

on the existing territorial roll will have the right to be registered, at his or her choice, on either of the new rolls'. The regulation covering this point provided that such persons should be placed on the higher roll unless they requested to be registered on the lower; it is not altogether clear why anyone should wish to do so, unless this was necessary for him to be a lower roll candidate, but the alternatives were offered because the 1956 requirements were lower than those for the new higher roll but higher than those for the lower. The U.F.P. also secured the right to a postal vote for persons on the higher roll.

A high proportion of the African population of Nyasaland spend much of their working life outside the country earning wages in the Rhodesias or the Union. Indeed the Nyasaland African Congress as a political movement was as strong in Southern Rhodesia as it was at home. The residence qualification was designed to take account of this movement in and out of the country. It required only that a voter should at the time of registration be ordinarily resident in the district where he applied for registration and should at any time in the past have been ordinarily resident in Nyasaland for any continuous period of two years; thus the more usual requirement of a period of residence immediately prior to registration was waived. The Malawi Party would have liked to see provision made to enable those who were out of the country at the time to register and vote, but apart from the practical difficulties that this would have involved, it was held that persons engaged on a labour contract in another territory could not be held to be 'ordinarily resident' in Nyasaland. Those who were at home for a period of leave in the course of an uncompleted labour contract were also not regarded as having the residence qualification.

In the 1956 elections postal voting had been allowed for the small scattered non-African electorate. The U.F.P. wished to retain this and the Malawi Party wanted postal voting to be general. The Working Party's view was that the controls necessary to prevent abuse would unduly complicate the electoral arrangements; they referred to the decision to abolish postal voting in Kenya. However, the U.F.P. secured from the Secretary of State the continuance of postal voting for the higher roll.

The method of calculating incomes and property presented special problems in the circumstances of Nyasaland. It was considered impossible to translate the value of subsistence agricultural production into cash, so that this could not be brought in as an item of an applicant's income; of course, it could never be enough to meet the qualification by itself. But payments in kind to employees (i.e. the value of board and lodging) were admissible; it seems that this provision was important largely in the case of missionaries.

Land held under customary tenure, and houses on such land, were not admitted as a property qualification, since they could not be said to have an assessable value.

It was agreed that no test of literacy should be imposed other than the requirement to fill in the application form unaided, and that in order to avoid confusing applicants by a large number of alternatives, different forms should be printed to suit the different categories. The languages recognized by the Working Party as current in Nyasaland were Nyanja, Yao, Tumbuka, Ngonde, Tonga and Gujerati. Urdu was added later on representations from Mr. Sattar Sacranie, who asserts that it is spoken by 15 per cent of the Asian population.

The Secretary of State's approval of the Working Party's report subject to the amendments described reached Zomba late on Christmas Eve. Legal provision to bring the recommendation into effect was made by an Order in Council of 21 December 1960,[1] which came into force on 31 December. The text of regulations[2] made under this Order in Council was shown to the Members of the Legislative Council on the same day and Order and Regulations were published on 3 January 1961. The U.F.P. maintained that they were not given reasonable time to consider them, but they succeeded in securing one amendment, namely that the re-registration of persons who had been registered for the 1956 election should be automatic. It is unlikely that this provision significantly increased the number of higher roll voters, but the automatic re-registration secured the retention on the roll of an unknown number of persons who may have been out of Nyasaland during the registration period or for other reasons found it inconvenient to register. Indeed, if it is true that many non-Africans thought it not worth the trouble of registering for an election in which an African majority in the Legislative Council was assured, this arrangement was of considerable significance. It placed on the registration officers the onus of checking which of the voters previously registered had changed their addresses, died or left the country, an addition to their burdens which they did not welcome. In assigning names to the appropriate electoral districts they had the additional difficulty that people living at some distance from the principal towns give as their addresses the post office boxes from which they collect their mail.

PREPARATIONS FOR REGISTRATION

At the time of the Lancaster House Conference Mr. Macleod had

[1] The Nyasaland (Electoral Provisions) (Amendment) Order in Council, 1960. S. I., 1960, No. 2414.
[2] The Legislative Council (Registration of Voters and Delimitation of Constituencies) Regulations 1961. Nyasaland Government Notice, No. 2.

B

suggested that the elections might be held in May 1961. The Malawi Congress Party received this suggestion with derision rather than indignation, asserting that they could perfectly well be held in November 1960. Hardly any members of the general public had any idea of the technical processes necessary for the organization of an election, or of the intervals between successive stages which are legally required, and the general view among Africans and their sympathizers was that delays were being contrived to put them at a disadvantage—to postpone the elections until after the Federation Review Conference, to give the U.F.P. more time to organize, to give Malawi time to disintegrate (as some of its African former members believed it would). The period for receiving claims and objections to registration was in fact increased by the Secretary of State from two to three weeks at the request of the U.F.P., who, it was thought, intended to contest a large number of registrations.

On 24 January the Deputy Chief Secretary announced at a press conference that the earliest possible date for the elections would be the end of July. Mr. Blackwood, then deputy leader of the U.F.P., welcomed the announcement on the ground that by that time the intimidation of political opponents might have been stopped; this gave Malawi spokesmen occasion to accuse the government of yielding to U.F.P. pressure.

Although the conditions of the franchise made automatic registration impossible, the government did not think that all initiative in stimulating voters to register must be left to the parties. An intensive preparatory campaign was organized by the Information Department. Posters and leaflets were distributed in English and the principal African languages, and information officers in loud-speaker vans toured the country announcing the significance of the registration and the qualifications required and answering questions. A vocabulary of English words used in connection with the election, with equivalents in three African languages, was published in a leaflet and was reproduced in *Malawi News*. U.F.P. supporters made some play with the fact that equivalents could not be found for 'vote' and 'voter', which were simply transliterated as so many English words have been in all African languages, but this did not become part of their official arguments against the liberal interpretation of the franchise regulations.

Altogether 136,000 leaflets were distributed by the Information Department, of which 10,000 were circulated with *Msimbi*, the Department's official newspaper; 60,000 were distributed by the touring information officers, and the remainder went to District Commissioners, Native Authorities and Registration Officers and to private persons who had applied to receive the Department's bulletins. The total number of different items printed in connection with the registration, including publicity material, supplements to the official gazette, instructions to registration officers and registration forms in different languages and applicable to people with different qualifications, was ninety-six, and the total of printed sheets of different kinds issued in connection with the registration reached a million.

The reversal of government policy implied in the release of Dr. Banda and the other detainees, the ending of the emergency and the Lancaster House Conference, left the Information Department in a somewhat embarrassing position. During the emergency its touring vans had been unpopular, not only as representing the government, but on account of the arguments in justification of the emergency regulations which it was their function to disseminate. Particularly in the Northern Province, where feeling had been highest before the emergency was declared, people wanted assurances of Dr. Banda's approval before they would listen to the information officers, and apparently this had not reached them a few days before the registration opened. (Nevertheless, registration in the north was high in relation to the total population.) It was reported that in the Central Province people were too busy planting their crops to gather around the loud-speaker vans. Near Blantyre I spent a morning with one Information Unit in a deluge of rain. It visited two Native Courts at which, the information officers told me, crowds might be expected, to find nobody there at all; an additional reason, however, was that the chiefs had not been told to expect it.

Posters were distributed by these touring vans, and were put up inside houses more often than outside. Some may have been torn down by Malawi supporters, though Malawi officially asked the Information Department to have printed on them the statement that it was an offence to deface them. I never saw a defaced poster. It is, however, possible that some people, such as store-owners, who were given posters for display were afraid to show them on account of the earlier attitude of Malawi towards anyone who co-operated with the government. An intelligent literate young man told me a few days before registration opened that he had seen no posters in Soche (the African township of Blantyre). It may be that in fact there were none displayed, but his remark suggests the difficulty of communicating in this impersonal way with people who are not conditioned to keep their eyes open for notices. Later, I saw a crowd outside a registration post which was not open that day; nobody present had thought to look at the notice giving the dates of opening. Of course, oral information was also given, not only by the Information Department but by administrative officers at meetings of chiefs and headmen.

The Information Units continued their tours during the registration period, at first making the normal announcement of the voting qualifications and waiting for questions, later simply calling on people to register and not delay. On one day's tour which I joined the questions asked were what people should do if they had lost their tax-receipts, and where a person should register if his home and place of work were different. At Lilongwe airport, where the van arrived at the staff quarters during working hours when only women were at home, the Information Officer improved the occasion by reminding them that they could qualify on the strength of their husbands' incomes. They replied that they did not know what their husbands earned, and indeed at one registration post I saw a couple come in together and the wife write 'no' against the question whether her husband had the qualifying income; but as he had given the appropriate income on his own form, this was not held to disqualify her from registering. A nice point which was difficult to explain was that all wives of a polygamist could qualify as married women, but only one could qualify in virtue of her husband's income; this was of little importance in practice, since the income qualification was significant in the main for salaried employees who were too young to qualify as ten-year tax-payers, and most of these would be unlikely at that age to have taken a second wife, even if they ever would. Another difficulty was the difference between the significance of a house as evidence of residence and as a property qualification, and, as might be expected, the difference between movable and immovable property and the fact that a herd of cattle or a store of grain could not be counted in reckoning up a citizen's worth were even harder to explain.

Quaint misunderstandings were many, and one had the impression that before the registration opened some people did not clearly distinguish it from the actual voting. Many thought that the registration process in some way committed their vote, and that the registration officers could draft them into the wrong party. The explanation given by one Malawi organizer for a low registration in his area was, 'someone is putting it about' that those who register will be committed to the U.F.P. Dr. Banda raised election funds by calling for a contribution of a shilling from each of his supporters. Instead of an ordinary receipt they got a little square of cardboard with 'Kamuzu's election shilling' printed on it, and some seem to have thought that this gave them the right to vote. An explanation of the requirement of ten years' payment of tax was interpreted in one place as an announcement that those who could produce the receipts would have their money refunded. Some people asked whether there would be separate registration posts for U.F.P. supporters, and others needed to be convinced that the election process was not something 'federal' and so to be boycotted by all good men. But the impression given by a good many comments was that the election was conceived not as a contest of which the outcome was, at least theoretically, in doubt, but as a sort of ritual demonstration of support for Dr. Banda.

THE REGISTRATION PERIOD

The registration period of four weeks opened on 13 February. The aim of the authorities was that nobody should have to go more than ten miles to a registration post, but this aim was not attained in the more sparsely populated areas, and some prospective voters came as much as twenty miles on foot. A figure of 350 posts was mentioned in January, but the actual number opened was 253. The calculation was that each should be able to register a hundred voters a day. Court houses, Native Authority offices, markets and the produce buying centres of the African Production and Marketing Board were used for the purpose; a few schools were used, but as far as possible this was avoided so as not to interfere with teaching. All District Offices had arrangements to deal with applications for registration at any time during their normal hours. For the convenience both of the administration and of voters, the registration posts were also to be the polling stations.

Malawi were extremely suspicious of the impartiality of government servants as registration officers, and Dr. Banda at one point suggested that the work should be done by persons from African territories outside Nyasaland. A less difficult proposal was that Nyasalanders not in government service should do it; this too was rejected on the ground that all such persons were involved with political parties. In addition to administrative officers, members of the technical departments—agriculture, forestry, education, treasury, public works, etc.—were appointed registration officers. District Commissioners as Chief Registration Officers were responsible for the general supervision of all posts in their districts. The number of posts in a district ranged from four in Blantyre Urban area to twenty-one in Lilongwe District. European registration officers numbered 168, Africans 50, and Asians 26.

District headquarters were open for registration during office hours throughout the period. Elsewhere registration posts were open at fixed hours or on fixed days, calculated in relation to the population to be served. The four posts in Blantyre and Limbe were open for two hours each morning and each afternoon. In the rural districts different posts were open on different days, the minimum being two periods of three days with an interval between them. Both in Blantyre and Limbe and in Lilongwe special times were set apart for the registration of Asian ladies.

The attitude of the Malawi Party was crucial to the success of the registration. Its members looked for instructions to Dr. Banda, and he gave these through the medium of *Malawi News*. He urged all qualified persons to register at the earliest possible moment, implying that the date of the elections would depend on the speed with which the registration was completed. With his principal lieutenants he attended a church service on the day before it opened to pray for its success.

Dr. Banda's lead, and his appeal for 'Peace and Calm', undoubtedly produced a *détente*, but he was careful not to appear to have relaxed his mistrust of the Nyasaland government (and, indeed, perhaps he had not done so). He took the line that officials were seeking excuses to suppress the party and its leaders, 'to provoke us into doing something stupid. Because they want us to cause trouble so that they can prevent elections from taking place'.[1]

Malawi organizers were in evidence at all registration posts, and during the first days had sometimes to be asked to stay outside the building. On balance, however, their contribution to the success of the proceedings was valuable. In some places they secured silence from noisy crowds, in others they formed the applicants into queues, dividing those who were not required to be literate from the rest; it is alleged that where this was done U.F.P. sympathisers found it was not possible for them to move up with the queue. In one district Malawi hired a lorry to bring supporters to registration posts; and in the same district they collected all the forms issued to applicants who had been refused registration, with the declared intention of contesting every refusal.

It appears that most of those who intended to register did so early in the four-week period. Where a registration post was opened for two spells with an interval between them, the numbers appearing at the second opening were noticeably fewer.

What surprised registration officers most was the long time spent in pondering over the forms by people who were in fact able to read them, as they showed by eventually completing the answers required. The instructions issued to registration officers indicated that they might supervise 'more than one' applicant at a time. Tables and ball-point pens were provided at first for four to six persons, but as time went on one began to see twenty or so sitting round a large table. Supervision was apparently adequate to prevent discussion between them, and it would seem safe to say that it would have been difficult for illiterate persons to copy from their neighbours without being observed. But

[1] *Malawi News*, 16 February 1961.

there were occasional surprising incidents, as when a whole batch of twenty answered 'No' to the question 'Are you male or female?'

Malawi organizers circulated cyclostyled copies of the application forms, in itself a perfectly admissible procedure, since they were published in the government gazette. They were said to have coached illiterate applicants to fill them. This must have been a man-power intensive industry in view of the fact that several of the answers required (name, tax assessment number *and* tax receipt number) were different in the case of every applicant. Coaching was suspected where answers were written opposite the wrong question; Malawi organizers treated this as the kind of mistake anyone might make, and indicated that they would challenge rejections based on this ground. Asian leaders made no secret of the fact that they had coached higher roll applicants in the correct English answers.

What took many Europeans by surprise was the realization that to people who do not spend their lives with pen in hand the filling up of a form is by no means a simple test. If literacy is the ability to recognize words on a page, it was undoubtedly possessed by many people who wrote quite silly answers. The young man who dealt with the question 'What is your occupation? Wives may insert "married" if they are not in paid employment' by copying the second sentence was not illiterate: he copied too fluently for that.

Some people were baffled by being asked what their sex was, a question to which they had always supposed the answer to be self-evident; more found difficulty in the declaration that they were not under allegiance to a foreign Power, a question which they are not likely to have contemplated before. Some simply found the small print was too much for them, and some spent so long pondering over it that eventually the registration authority sent them home and told them to try again next day. It may be that some were discouraged from making the second attempt, but no one who observed the conduct of the registration could fail to be impressed by the patience of those in charge towards the slower performers. Most registration posts were open for much longer than the times announced.

Registration officers were, of course, debarred from giving applicants any help of a kind that would enable them to disguise illiteracy. Where an applicant left a question unanswered, they did not reject him out of hand but indicated the omission, and they were allowed to strike out such questions as need not be answered, particularly those asked of women only. They were empowered to help blind or disabled persons. In the case of the former some indication was sought that they had once been literate, for example by asking what schooling they had had. A difficult problem was that of people who could see their way about but said their eyes were not good enough to read print, and could well be speaking the truth in a country where few people have benefit of oculists. In one or two places the provision that disabled persons could be helped was taken by the public to mean that anyone could ask a registration officer to help him.

At one or two posts, applicants who were clearly not qualified were weeded out from the queues outside by the registration officer's African clerk; this was of course interpreted by Malawi as a deliberate means of preventing their supporters from registering. At the central post in Blantyre the clerk stood outside the door repeating the qualifications, but did not ask any questions of individuals.

In view of all the discussion of the women's vote, it is perhaps not surprising that this was the subject of much misunderstanding; apparently a good many women did not know that they had to be literate. On an early registration day in Limbe, about fifty women turned up, of whom only six proved to be qualified. Later the admission to registration of the one or two women Native Authorities gave rise to a rumour that all wives of chiefs were entitled to the vote. *Malawi News*[1] complained that women were being prevented from registering; a total of 10,000 did so, however.

Registration officers were instructed that 'the object of the exercise is to register voters', and although they were also instructed that they could not vary the regulations, they did not use excessive rigour in demanding evidence of qualifications. The production of the previous year's tax receipt was taken as *prima facie* evidence that an applicant had paid all the taxes for which he was liable, since a receipt is not issued unless any arrears have been paid. If he seemed to be under 28, registration officers were instructed to check his name in the tax register, but, as has been explained, some districts did not have records going back ten years. Some applicants were asked what the rate of tax was when they first paid, a question to which it was easy to give the right answer.

In districts where the registration of marriages is compulsory (in order to enable migrant labourers to claim married quarters, transport for their wives, etc.) women were expected to produce the certificate; elsewhere they were supposed to bring a letter from their village headman. In practice, it seems that in case of doubt the headman or some other senior neighbour was usually present and could be appealed to.

In most rural areas all applicants filled up their forms in the local language. In Blantyre all the admissible languages were offered, and some more, so that all the different forms were in use. Provision was made for forms completed in Indian languages to be checked by appropriate persons. I heard an old man ask to write his application in

[1] 2 March.

'Islam', which may have meant Yao in Arabic characters; he was not understood.

The checking of claims based on income, or on the educational standards required for the higher roll, was more complicated. There was little difficulty where the income came from a salary; what was interesting here was that applicants often seemed to need help in calculating whether their monthly earnings added up to the required annual income. Self-employed persons were more difficult to deal with; at one post it was suggested that they ought to be asked to produce an accountant's certificate. In the main, however, registration officers relied on the applicants' good faith unless they had serious reason to doubt it.

The measurement of the educational levels required to qualify for the higher roll was difficult in the case of people who had been to school at a time before current systems of grading had been established. However, for younger candidates the registration officers had a list of the school grades in every territory in South, East and Central Africa, as well as the certificates of correspondence colleges, which were to be treated as equivalent to primary and secondary education as defined in Nyasaland. Applicants only had to have been 'exposed to' education of this grade, no standard of achievement was required; that is, they must have entered for examinations at the appropriate stage, but need not have passed them. Indian equivalents were not given; this may well have been impossible. I met an Asian schoolmaster who complained that he had been 'insulted' at the previous registration because he could not produce evidence of his schooling in India, and seemed to be reluctant for this reason to apply again.

An unexpected difficulty was the appearance of rival claimants to village headmanships—in one case as many as five. The division of villages, which is always going on, is not recognized by the administration, to whom a village is the aggregate of tax-payers registered in a single volume. Usually this question was settled by demanding the production of the 'tax-book'.

The reluctance of Asians to register was a matter of concern to their leaders. It was explained in general terms by political apathy and the desire to avoid involvement. Mr. Sacranie, their leader, visited Lilongwe for the express purpose of urging them to register. In Limbe, Asian store-owners said they could not leave their businesses to stand in queues. Here Mr. Sacranie organized parties of young men to look after a shop for a morning.

The Lancaster House agreement was reached in August. The rainy season in Nyasaland normally begins in November, so that it would barely have been possible to make the necessary preparations in time to get the registration over first. Heavy rain naturally deterred people from walking long distances to stand in long queues, and occasionally made it impossible for people to get to the registration posts; in some areas the period was extended for five days to allow for this. The total number of voters when registration closed on 18 March was 107,076 on the lower roll and 4,401 on the higher. 597 Asians, including 47 women, registered on the lower roll, and 16 Europeans. Altogether there were 10,185 lower roll women voters. On the higher roll there were 2,895 Europeans, 1,035 Asians and 471 Africans. 15,600 were in the categories not required to be literate; 10,132 of these were chiefs, councillors or village headmen.

Four weeks were allowed for the compilation of registers. In the case of the lower roll the Nyasaland authorities had an advantage over some other organizers of elections in dependent territories, namely that in African townships all houses are numbered and in the rural areas every taxpayer is identified by a number on the tax register. Applicants for registration were asked to give this number with their other particulars (if they did not know it they were entitled to have the registration officer look it up for them.) The villages in each district were also numbered, so that registers could be compiled in which any voter could be easily identified without the necessity of searching through several hundred Abdullas or Keitas which has faced polling officers elsewhere. The U.F.P. did not avail themselves of the extended period for raising objections to registration, and the number of claims to have been omitted was extremely small except in Kasungu, where enthusiastic Malawi organizers collected the names of 159 persons who had been refused registration. Eight of these were held to have valid claims. Only fifty-five claims were received from the rest of the country.

PREPARATIONS FOR POLLING

Further regulations[1] dealing with the qualifications of candidates and the conduct of the elections were published on 20 March. Candidates were required to be 25 years of age and be registered voters, to have been ordinarily resident in Nyasaland for periods amounting in the aggregate to two years out of the four preceding the election (this would enable persons to stand who had been employed outside the Protectorate) and to satisfy the Speaker that their knowledge of English was adequate for them to take part in the proceedings of the legislature. Those whose mother tongue was English, who had the degree of a University where teaching was given in English, or who had previously been members of Legislative Council, were not required to give further

[1] The Legislative Council (Elections) Regulations 1961.

evidence that they were qualified on this count. Others had to obtain a certificate to that effect from a Provincial Education Officer, on the basis of a standard test provided by the Speaker. The test was to read a passage from Hansard, answer questions the answers to which were contained in the passage, and comment on it in writing. Only four prospective candidates failed to pass. After debate in the Legislative Council it was agreed that a candidate might stand on either roll, no matter on which he was registered, provided he had the qualifications of a voter on the roll in which he stood. The deposit required was £15 for the lower and £50 for the higher roll.

The provision debarring government servants from candidature was not held to cover members of the armed forces, special constabulary or police reserve, members or employees of Native Authorities, or employees of other types of local authority. Persons disqualified from standing included those 'detained under a detention order or subject to a control or restriction order'. This provision did not affect any potential candidates at the 1961 election. One of them, Mr. Chipembere, was in prison, but not under a detention order; he had been convicted of a criminal offence.

Since all lower roll voters were not required to be literate, the polling method adopted for the lower roll was that of multiple ballot boxes distinguished by symbols. Provision was also made for the display outside the polling station of a notice giving in English and the principal local language the names, addresses, occupations and symbols of the candidates, and of notices both inside and outside instructing voters how to vote.

European members of the Legislative Council objected to the allocation of symbols to parties and not to individuals, arguing that this concentrated attention on the party rather than the candidate. They also described the voting methods as an insult to Africans, and suggested that it would be preferable to have voting papers marked with a rubber stamp or thumb-print opposite the candidate's symbol. All the abuses possible under the multiple box system were enumerated. The system is also criticized by psephologists, partly because simpler alternatives have in practice been found possible but also because of the opportunities which it gives for the smuggling of ballot papers. Some West African regulations have permitted the searching of voters when they leave the polling booth, and it is said that this has been an effective deterrent. In Sierra Leone, where there was no such provision, there was a single conviction for this offence. With a large electorate smuggling must be done on a considerable scale to affect the issue. Where the total numbers are as small as they were in Nyasaland a few smuggled ballots could have a significant effect. But for organized smuggling to be practicable there must be a number of indifferent voters who are amenable to offers from party agents but cannot be trusted to use their votes themselves in the desired way. This proved not to be the case.

The Supervisor of Elections was required, immediately after the delimitation of constituencies, to divide each one into polling divisions, in each of which there should normally be a single polling station. The regulations did not assign responsibility for the siting of polling stations, but it had been intended from the outset that they should be the same buildings that had been used for the registration. No stipulations were made as to the form of the polling booth. Polling hours were to be from 6.30 a.m. to 5.30 p.m.

The regulation covering the issue of ballot papers contained the usual provision that the voter's registration number should be written on the counterfoil, though this has been found in other cases to take up a good deal of time, to be done sometimes so inefficiently as to be useless for its ostensible purpose, and to lead the voters to doubt the secrecy of the ballot.

The regulations dealing with corrupt practices included one devised for the special circumstances of Nyasaland, which included under the heading of 'undue influence' threats 'to inflict . . . by any supernatural or non-natural means or pretended supernatural or non-natural means any temporal or spiritual injury, damage, harm or loss'.

Information on the number of voters registered at each registration sub-district was compiled in advance of the detailed registers, for the benefit of the commission appointed to delimit the constituencies. This information was also sent to the headquarters of all political parties and to the offices of all Provincial and District Commissioners.

A schedule to the Regulations published in January asked the delimitation commissioners to 'give due consideration' to a number of matters. The first of these were, in fact, instructions: the boundaries of lower roll constituencies should not cross the boundaries either of Native Authority areas or of Provinces, and where practicable should not cross those of Districts. Where practicable, the same principles should be followed in delimiting higher roll constituencies in rural areas. On the other matters listed the commissioners were not given any explicit lead. They were asked to take into consideration 'the delimitation of urban constituencies where there is a high density of higher franchise voters within the main urban areas'; 'in each constituency there should, if possible, be some community of interest among the potential voters and among the population generally'; 'means of communication within each constituency'; 'sparsity or density of registered voters within each constituency'; and 'the possibility of aligning the boundaries of a higher franchise constituency with those of one or more lower franchise constituencies where such appears desirable'.

Malawi argued that the constituency boundaries should be drawn to equalize total population, not registered voters, since these would be the spokesmen of the voteless—an interesting interpretation of the principle 'one vote, one value' where it is not combined with 'one man, one vote'.

The Commission consisted of Sir Charles Hartwell, Chairman of the Public Service Commission of Northern Rhodesia, Mr. G. Hucks, clerk to the Legislative Council of Tanganyika, and Mr. Lewis Bandawe, a retired Nyasaland civil servant. They began work on 8 April, and their report was issued on 20 May.[1]

On the lower roll there were eight constituencies in the Southern Province with its total of 39,178 voters, seven in the Central Province with 38,609 and five in the Northern with 28,308. The Southern Province constituencies included the administrative districts of Zomba (5,985), Mlanje (7,748), Blantyre Urban (4,046) and Cholo (4,820). Chikwawa and Port Herald were combined to give a total of 4,618 voters; Kasupe and Fort Johnston to give a total of 4,429. Blantyre Rural, with a total registration of 8,000, was divided into the two constituencies of Blantyre Rural (4,074) and Chiradzulu (3,948). In the Central Province Lilongwe, with its total of 9,628 voters, was divided into a northern and a southern constituency, the latter, with 5,047 voters, including the township. Fort Manning was joined to Kasungu, giving a total of 8,166. The other districts had one seat each: Dedza (5,667), Dowa (6,449), Kota Kota (4,311) and Ncheu (4,434). In the Northern Province, Mzimba with its 13,802 registered voters was divided in two, with 7,723 and 6,137 voters respectively. The other three districts each formed one constituency: Rumpi (3,620), Karonga (5,623) and Nkata Bay (5,650).

Of the eight higher roll constituencies, the Northern Province, with 326 registered voters, was one. The Central Province had two— Lilongwe Town (327) and the rest (467). In the Southern Province, where there were 3,281 out of the total higher roll registration of 4,401, there were five constituencies. One, Shire North, combined the three districts of Fort Johnston, Kasupe and Zomba, with a total of 593 voters. One combined Cholo, Mlanje, Chikwawa and Port Herald, with 567.

The Blantyre area presented some difficulties. For the lower roll seats it had been divided into the two administrative districts, Blantyre Urban and Blantyre Rural. These together included over 2,000 of the total of

[1] Report of the Constituencies Commission, Zomba, 1961.

4,401 higher roll voters. As represented by the registration they were very unevenly distributed. Blantyre Rural had only 82 higher roll voters. Of the four registration sub-districts in Blantyre Urban, two had nearly 900 each, the other two just over 900. The Commission proposed the division of the whole area into three constituencies, Blantyre, Soche and Limbe, with approximately equal numbers of voters. The division cut across the boundaries of the district and sub-districts that had been used for registration purposes, and it was recognized that some adjustment would have to be made for voters who now found themselves on the register of a constituency where they neither lived, worked nor owned property. When the re-adjustment was made it was found that there was still a marked inequality between Blantyre with 411 voters and Soche with 996. A further boundary adjustment was made which reduced the voting population of Soche to 773 and increased that of Blantyre to 644, incidentally increasing the number of non-European voters in Blantyre. Each of the three constituencies included a densely populated urban area and a part of Blantyre Rural district in which a few higher roll voters were widely scattered.

Both the Information Department and Malawi were active in making the African public familiar with the rules and process of voting, and both deserve great credit for the remarkably smooth and orderly conduct of the polling. A film illustrating the voting process was shown all over the country, posters were displayed emphasizing the secrecy of the vote, and questions asked of touring information teams were collected and broadcast with appropriate answers.

Malawi, possibly with Ghana in mind, chose a cock as their symbol. The Christian Liberation Party had a cross and an eagle. The U.F.P. symbol, the leopard, is also part of the arms of Nyasaland, where it appears in front of a rising sun. This choice did lead Africans to ask whether the U.F.P. had government backing; it also made it necessary to paint out the leopard which adorned the Information Department landrovers.

As July approached new reasons arose for postponing the election date. The government decided to pass a budget before dissolving the legislature; for this purpose a session had to be held in the first week of July. The earliest possible date for nominations was now 20 July. The government intended to fix polling day at the end of the legal minimum period of three weeks from nomination day, but the U.F.P. protested that this was not long enough for postal voters in the United Kingdom, and asked for an additional week. The compromise finally reached was that polling should take place on 15 August.

The polling stations were the same solid buildings which had been used for registration. The ballot boxes were placed at one end of the building, with a screen of sacking or grass surrounding them on three sides. The difficulty reported from other territories, of making the screen thick enough to conceal the voter without making the interior too dark for him to see what he was doing, did not arise here, and one wonders why it ever need if the voting booth is not roofed over. The boxes were placed as close together as possible so that no conclusions could be drawn from the number of steps taken by the voter before he paused to insert his paper.

2. THE PARTIES

THE NYASALAND AFRICAN CONGRESS

The African parties all stemmed from one original source, the Nyasaland African Congress founded in 1944. This organization grew out of the activities of welfare associations of African civil servants in several District headquarters, which combined in a territory-wide body with the sympathy and support of official and missionary circles. Its first conference, in 1944, was addressed by the Governor. At this early stage Congress began to assert its claim to be recognized as the body representative of African interests in matters of general policy. The official reply to this was that the Protectorate Council, consisting of representatives of the Provincial Councils,[1] was the recognized mouthpiece of African opinion; the later inclusion in the Council of persons other than chiefs gave an opportunity for Congress members to take part in its discussions, but here they continued to be a minority in a body of a much more conservative character.

The original aims of the Congress were to secure better educational facilities for Africans in order to enable them to take their share in government, and 'general economic development, better farming and Urban Commerce and Industries'. In 1947 it sent a delegation to Britain to press for opportunities for higher education; the delegation sought the assistance of Dr. Banda, who was then practising medicine in London, and Congress appointed him its adviser in the United Kingdom. Congress espoused the interests of the tenants on estates in the Southern Province, whose grievances were the subject of a special inquiry in 1946, and supported the demands for the return of land held by missions which were being made at that time.

Its history in the years immediately preceding the declaration of a

[1] See pp. 7-8.

state of emergency in March 1959 is summarized in the Devlin Commission's report.[1] It was opposed from the outset to federation with the Rhodesias, for reasons closely similar to those that a generation earlier had led the Africans in Uganda to oppose 'Closer Union'—the expectation that this would lead to the domination of Europeans in an independent government, and this in turn to the alienation of African lands. Congress also feared the extension to Nyasaland of the colour bar as Nyasaland Africans had experienced it in the Rhodesias.

A non-violent resistance movement was organized when the federal constitution came into force in 1953. This had the support of some Native Authorities, notably the respected Ngoni chief Gomani. The removal of Gomani from office led to some disturbances, and other riots later in the year were suppressed with some loss of life. After this, Congress abandoned organized action, though it continued to assert its opposition to federation.

In 1956 the electoral colleges for the five African seats were the supposedly conservative Provincial Councils. Nevertheless, all the successful candidates were members of Congress, and the two who gained the largest majorities were young men under thirty, Mr. H. B. Chipembere and Mr. W. K. Chiume, the one an African District Assistant, the other a former student of Makerere University College. The other three, Messrs. Chinyama, Chijozi and Kwenje, were of an older generation.[2] The division of Congress into a right and a left wing soon became evident. A close association developed between the two left-wing members and Mr. D. K. Chisiza, another young man whom Chipembere described in a letter to Dr. Banda as a 'self-made intellectual . . . who surprises us all with his mental powers';[3] this estimate is endorsed by European sympathisers with the nationalist movement. Chipembere and Chiume secured his appointment as organizing secretary of Congress.

It was the left wing, and notably Chipembere, who considered that what the party needed was a charismatic leader, but that he must be a man whose standing would in itself command prestige. Dr. Hastings Banda was clearly the man, and after he had been persuaded to lead a delegation to the Secretary of State with proposals for constitutional change, he agreed to return to Nyasaland and head the party. He arrived there in July 1958, and on 1 August was elected President-General of Congress at its annual meeting. All Congress leaders agreed that he should have authority to appoint the executive committee and

[1] *Report of the Nyasaland Commission of Inquiry*, Cmnd. 814, 1959.
[2] *See* Colin Leys, 'An Election in Nyasaland', *Political Studies*, vol. v, 1957, pp. 258–80.
[3] Quoted in Cmnd. 814, p. 14.

all officers of the party; it is said now that he controls appointments even to the innumerable branch committees. His choice fell upon the younger men, Chipembere becoming treasurer, Chiume publicity secretary and Chisiza secretary-general. He added to the organization of the party a Women's League and a Youth League. The former combines activities of a women's institute type with the raising of funds; members of its branches are sometimes to be seen walking along the roads in formation and singing the songs in praise of Dr. Banda which in part fulfil the function of party slogans. They turn out as a body to greet Dr. Banda at his public appearances. The president of the Women's League is a member of the Executive Council of the party, and according to its leading officials there is a branch wherever the party has a branch. The members elect their own committees, and two delegates from each branch elect a committee for each district. There is obviously a special need for women's organizations in a country where women do not normally associate with men in public activities. The Women's League was made responsible for securing the registration of women as voters in the 1961 election. It is sometimes called the Amazon Army.

The Youth League, for members under thirty, is not closely comparable to the young members' organizations of British political parties; indeed an anthropologist might see a closer parallel in the age-regiments of some African societies, though these are not characteristic of the Nyasaland peoples. An incautious speaker once described it to me as 'our army', and it has been responsible not only for such harmless necessary activities as carrying messages, but for picketing roads and 'policing' areas where Congress was strong, and has probably taken its share in the acts of violence which preceded the declaration of the emergency; of course it is impossible to differentiate in a crowd between young men who conceive themselves to be furthering political aims and the 'hooligan element'.

The instructions issued to Youth League members when the election campaign opened indicate what were officially regarded as its functions at that time. They were reminded that the League had been formed to prepare the party leaders of the future. First they were required 'strictly to obey instructions', which come from the Great Kamuzu himself. They were to see that all meetings were made known in advance, to keep order at them and look after material arrangements ('platforms, if there are to be any, must be of a first-class nature and well looked after'). They must arrange for people who could not walk to meetings to be carried in hammocks.[1] They must organize bands and dance companies

---

[1] I never saw this happen, nor did I see voters carried to polling stations, though this appeared to be expected.

on a large scale. They must teach the general public 'all political issues, all current instructions'. They were also responsible for 'organizing, propagating, campaigning and publicity'. They must bring 'the whole three million people in Malawi' within the paid membership of the party. They must accompany high party officials on their tours and be available to carry messages 'and to look to the general security of the whole party'.

A feature of the Youth League branches which appears to be peculiar to the Northern Province is that they offer their work to farmers for pay which is contributed to party funds.

The African Chamber of Commerce, a body founded in 1953, in the nature of things consisted of Congress supporters. Its founder, Mr. Mikeka Mkandawire, was the owner of a bar in Soche. In 1958 Dr. Banda requested him 'to reform the Chamber so that African businessmen and women could be organized',[1] but little was done until after the ending of the emergency. In 1960, it was re-organized and Coloured traders were invited to join it; their leader, Mr. I. K. Surtee, who has a business in Balaka, became a member of the committee. Dr. Banda made the Chamber responsible for organizing registration on the higher roll. They were reported to have a committee of eight in every district, and paid organizing secretaries. In June 1961 they moved into the former offices of the Malawi Congress Party.

A trade union organization, the Nyasaland Council of Labour, was in general sympathy with Malawi aims but unlike its counterpart in Ghana was not regarded as an arm of the party. Its leaders made pronouncements on nationalization which were in direct contradiction with the Malawi policy of encouraging foreign investment.

With Dr. Banda's return the aims of Congress took shape in the form in which they are now inscribed over the office of its successor, the Malawi Congress Party, 'Independence and Secession Now'. Indeed many of Dr. Banda's pronouncements were characterized by a certain merging of the present and future tenses which may well have confused his followers. They were so often told that Kamuzu has 'got self-government' and that 'federation is dead' that they were acting only logically when they asserted that they would obey only their own police and not the government's. One of their European sympathizers stated more than once in print that Dr. Banda was in fact in power; but this was to ignore the dependence of a modern government on its administrative employees.

Congress now returned to the idea of a non-co-operation movement as a way of putting pressure on the government to secure the constitutional advances which it demanded—in essence an African majority in

[1] *Nyasaland Forum*, 30 May 1961.

both Legislative and Executive Councils. In this matter it seems clear that there was a difference in outlook between Dr. Banda and his young lieutenants, who favoured active violence, in particular attacks on Africans in the service of government, as well as passive resistance. Parallel with this is the difference in the general impression created by the public statements of Dr. Banda and Mr. Chipembere about future relations with Europeans. Although the former made demagogic speeches in which the keynote was the epithet 'stupid' applied to the federation and to any individuals who supported it and opposed the aims of Congress, he frequently referred to the country's need for Europeans and his own intention of co-operating with them. This was the gist of his last public speech before his arrest; the corresponding one by Chipembere is reported to have contained a statement that 'every European is the enemy of every African in Nyasaland'.[1] Nevertheless Dr. Banda's African opponents sought to make capital out of his own alleged expressions of hatred for Europeans.[2]

THE MALAWI CONGRESS PARTY

The new policy led quickly enough to the declaration of a state of emergency, the outlawing of Congress as a party and the arrest of over a thousand persons. The resurrection of the party under another name was inevitable, as was the eventual release of its leaders, but in fact this took place at the end of 1959 while the most conspicuous members were still in detention. It was inspired by a young man of remarkable intelligence, Mr. Aleke Banda,[3] who, like other Congress supporters in Salisbury, was sent home when the emergency was declared. He occupied his time preparing as an external candidate for the examinations that he had been working for at school, and when Mr. Orton Chirwa, Nyasaland's only African lawyer, was released Aleke Banda went to him and proposed that he should lead a new party, the Malawi Congress Party, modelled closely on the old, with its life president, its executive committee, its provincial and area committees and its Women's League and Youth League. The name is that of an ancient African kingdom geographically somewhere near the present Nyasaland, which had already been used by Dr. Banda. In the popular mind its most important aims were 'secession and independence now' and 'one man, one vote'. Neither of these appears in the statement of aims which heads the undated copy of the party constitution given me at headquarters.[4]

[1] *Pretoria News*, 28 February 1959, quoted *Africa Digest*, vol. vi, p. 172.
[2] Cf. *Nyasaland Forum*, 6 June 1961.
[3] No relation to the Doctor; the name is one of the commonest in Nyasaland.
[4] *See* Appendix I.

According to the constitution the membership of the Party was to consist of individuals and affiliated organizations. Its highest authority was the annual delegates conference, consisting of 'delegates appointed by the branches'. A branch must have at least ten members. All branches in a district formed the 'District Party' which must meet once monthly. Provincial Parties, not defined, must meet quarterly. Provincial chairmen were to be elected annually from candidates approved by the central executive. The constitution refers to Provincial District and Branch Executives but does not lay down their composition or method of appointment.

The President was to be elected by the annual conference for a period of three years and be re-eligible. He was to be advised by a central executive consisting, apparently,[1] of ten persons elected by the Provincial Committees and ten elected by the annual conference.

A national committee, consisting of one representative from each district, elected from candidates approved by the central executive, was to meet half-yearly to receive a report from the central executive on the implementation of policy decided on at the annual conference.

As it was illegal to hold meetings the new party was organized by the distribution of circulars, sometimes by post, sometimes by hand, for example to passengers in buses, but also by runners paid to go through the country. In two months Orton Chirwa had collected enough money to finance a visit to London to see the Secretary of State, and when he arrived in London he claimed a membership of 17,000.

The party then bought a duplicating machine and began to publish a weekly journal, *Malawi News*, edited by Aleke Banda. In February 1961 it acquired its own printing press, and the paper began to appear in printed form. It normally had six pages, four in English and one in each of the two leading African languages. In July it began to appear twice weekly as a four-page sheet.

Most of its space was given to political events in Nyasaland, but nationalist movements in other African territories were also discussed. There was a satirical commentary by 'Professor Ludicrous', and the earlier numbers carried a series by Orton Chirwa explaining the principles of a representative constitution.

A monthly journal of comment, *Tsopano* [*Now*], was launched by two European sympathizers during the emergency period and before the founding of the Malawi Party. This carried biographical articles on leading Nyasalanders, a sort of 'This England' column recording instances of injustice to Africans, and correspondence. In dealing with events on which there was controversy as to the facts, the African version was given. The editor hoped that this might become a forum for

[1] The text is by no means clear.

the serious discussion of policy questions. It was handed over to the same management as *Malawi News* in February 1961, but did not appear between this date and the elections.

The new party held its first annual congress at Kota Kota in September 1960, after the last detainees had been released. Chipembere and Chisiza returned to their offices of treasurer-general and secretary-general respectively. Dr. Banda was now elected life president, and shortly afterwards the party presented him with a house on the outskirts of Blantyre, which is always referred to as the presidential palace. No meetings of the national committee appear to have been held.

At the Kota Kota meeting Dr. Banda formally denounced violence and Chipembere added that 'now that Kamuzu had achieved self-government' there was no further need for it. It then became the party line that all accusations of violence were false, and in the minds of some members this view was retrospective. Mrs. Rose Chibambo, the Women's League President, who had a right to a grievance in that when she was arrested she had to leave her young children alone, assured me that 'we have been peaceful throughout'. If violence is committed against members of parties opposed to Malawi, this is a sinister device of the opponents for discrediting Malawi. Certainly the opponents, particularly Europeans, have made the most of cases of intimidation; but one must be completely blinded by partisanship to believe that there never were any.

Since the end of the emergency conspicuous acts of violence—mostly the burning of houses—have been directed not against persons in government employment but against those who have joined opposition parties, and few people can believe that these are matters of pure coincidence. Dr. Banda has repeatedly denounced such acts, but the burning of Mr. Chester Katsonga's house followed so closely upon the 'Kill Europeans' speech for which Chipembere was eventually sentenced to three years' imprisonment that it is hard to dissociate the two events. This happened while Dr. Banda was in London for the federation review conference, and led him to return in a hurry and discipline his lieutenant, who had referred in the same speech to what 'Chiume and he' would do when the country was independent.

Some observers ascribed the much greater calm of 1961 to the stiff sentences passed on disturbers of the peace. But the most conspicuous trials were not held till half-way through February, and there had been a marked decrease in acts of violence before this. At least equal credit must be given to Dr. Banda's stand.

It is harder to make a firm judgment on the extent of subtler forms of intimidation. Forms of social pressure such as boycott are practised in most societies against people who deviate from strongly held norms;

and for Malawi members support of the party *is* a moral norm, not just a matter of opinion. A boycott can destroy the livelihood of an African trader, but it is not a legal offence. The subtlest form of intimidation in the literal sense of causing fear is the 'wait and see' type of threat that to Africans carries the implication of revenge by occult means, and even sometimes of occult knowledge of the way people have voted in a secret ballot. Nobody can tell how many people have been influenced by such threats. But it is my impression that the fear which prevailed before the emergency had no counterpart during the election period.

Officially, the difference between Dr. Banda and Chipembere was over tactics, not over leadership. The party line, of course, was that there had been no question of a contest for leadership. Yet an order was issued after Dr. Banda's return that no names other than his were to be mentioned in party songs. The party financed Chipembere's defence and his appeal, and maintained that his conviction was unfair. Yet it may well be that the election period would have been more disturbed if he had taken part in the campaign, and that this might have caused embarrassment to his leader. Some observers foresee that he may yet re-appear to challenge Dr. Banda's position with a more uncompromising policy.

In November 1960 Malawi claimed a million and a half members paying an annual subscription of two shillings. They rely less on regular subscriptions, however, than on *ad hoc* levies, which usually bring in considerable sums. They have also received contributions from Ghana. Branches do not manage their own funds. All sums collected are paid in to the headquarters, and when a large meeting is to be organized, the branch concerned applies there for the money it needs for such purposes as hiring lorries to bring the audience from a distance.

Early in February the national headquarters was set up in a large building in Limbe, a few hundred yards, as it happened, from the headquarters office of the United Federal Party. This contained a printing press as well as the offices of the treasurer, secretary-general, publicity secretary and editor of *Malawi News*. At the time of the elections the party had nineteen cars of various kinds, perhaps the most important requirement for a political campaign in a tropical territory. Six land-rovers were presented by Mr. Julius Nyerere after Malawi complained that agents in Salisbury had refused to supply them 'for political reasons'.[1]

Dr. Banda expressed views on specific matters of policy on various occasions before the election period. He did not believe that the poverty of Nyasaland was in fact a serious problem, but held, on the contrary, that intensive agricultural development could quickly turn it into a

[1] *African Weekly*, 22 February.

'Central African Denmark'. According to Mr. Aleke Banda, this implied the use of ploughs, the re-allocation of land and the improvement
of cultivation by propaganda without the imposition of penalties. Dr.
Banda proposed to make agriculture a compulsory school subject. He
believed, like most of his followers, that the country contained undis-
covered mineral resources. He allowed that it might be desirable to
associate with neighbouring territories, but that this must be done by
the free choice of the people. On a visit to London in April 1961 he was
reported as saying that once 'this stupid federation' had been got rid of
he might be willing to discuss some other form of closer association
even with the Rhodesias, but on his return to Nyasaland he indignantly
denied this report, and recalled that he and Mr. Nyerere had issued a
joint statement of their intention of entering into a political union which
would form 'a nucleus of a greater union of East and Central African
territories'. He also denied that business men in Britain or America had
suggested that they would be more inclined to invest in Nyasaland if it
remained within the federation. *Malawi News* reported a lunch in
London with the Nyasaland Tea Association, at which Dr. Banda said
that he would welcome investors and would create such conditions as
would assure the security of their investments. He also announced proposals to found a university, greatly to expand women's education, and
to increase facilities for sport. To the accusations of the Christian
Liberation Party he retorted that Malawi is the party of Christians.

Other party aims were deducible from statements that appeared in
comment or other features in *Malawi News*. Particularly significant
were passages in Orton Chirwa's series of articles on parliamentary
government. In discussing cabinet government he remarked that the
Lancaster House constitution fell short of this and 'owing to the delay
in the implementation of the agreement' was already out of date; the
mixed executive council could not be expected to last more than six
months. In a later article he emphasized the need for an efficient civil
service with promotion dependent on merit alone.

Dr. Banda's statement on his return from America in May had some
of the characteristics of an election programme. He enumerated a
number of schemes which he said he had discussed when in the United
States, and for which 'money would pour into the country from
America, Britain, Holland, Germany and other countries'. These included the construction of a lake-side road from Fort Johnston to
Karonga; the resuscitation of the Shire Highlands hydro-electric
scheme; the development of processing industries; and the creation of a
university, to be inspired by the ideals of Dr. Robert Laws but planned
by an American committee.

The divisions within the Congress (and later Malawi) Party have been divisions between the right and left wing, which in fact correspond to the older and younger generation. All were agreed on opposition to federation and on the ultimate aim of independence for Nyasaland as an African state, but the older members were willing to co-operate with the official element in the existing legislature to an extent that Chiume regarded as 'fraternizing with imperialists'.[1] The correspondent of the *Economist* shortly after the 1956 election described Congress plans to form a 'shadow cabinet'. This may be what Chiume refers to in his article as a Parliamentary Committee of which Chinyama refused to be chairman because he thought it would be considered subversive.

THE ASIAN CONVENTION

Something must be said of an organization that was neither a political party nor an organ of the M.C.P., though it gave its full support to Malawi: the Asian Convention. Up to 1952 the only Asian organization was the Chamber of Commerce. In that year the Convention was founded by Mr. Sattar Sacranie to express the opposition of Asians to the federation. During the short period when one of the unofficial seats in the Legislative Council was allotted to an Asian Mr. Sacranie was nominated to it. But by the time of Dr. Banda's return the Asians as a whole, like their fellows in other African territories, had come to think that their future lay in amicable relations with the African majority rather than in any demand for special representation or other safeguards. At Lancaster House Mr. Sacranie supported Dr. Banda and during the election period he pledged the Asian vote to Malawi; he also announced that the Asian Convention would shortly be disbanded, leaving no exclusively Asian organization.

THE BREAKAWAY PARTIES

The first open division of opinion within Congress occurred when Chiume and Chipembere in December 1956 proposed to the Executive Council that the two Nyasaland African members of the federal legislature be called on to resign. This was opposed by 'all the recognized leaders' and the motion was lost by six votes to thirty-six. In May 1957, however, the left-wing policy prevailed, and a letter was sent to them asking them to resign their seats. They refused to do so, and in this had the support of the three older Legislative Council members. They were then formally expelled from Congress.

Mr. T. D. T. Banda, the President-General of Congress at the time when this decision was taken, was himself expelled from Congress in 1958 after being accused of malversation of funds, a charge which he

---

[1] *Malawi News*, 30 March 1961.

told the Devlin Commission had been trumped up. The Commission refers to a report that he and Mr. Wellington Chirwa, one of the federal M.P.s, were 'getting together'. Another explanation offered is that Dr. Banda made the removal of Mr. T. D. T. Banda a condition of his return. Mr. Banda had a personal following in Cholo and Chiradzulu, where he had been active in espousing the cause of African tenants on alienated land, and in his home district of Nkata Bay. Members of the Cholo branch of Congress, led by their chairman, Mr. Kamwana, urged him to form a new party.

This was the Congress Liberation Party, which in 1961 repudiated unconstitutional action but claimed at the same time to be more sincere and uncompromising in its opposition to federation than Dr. Banda himself. As C.L.P. officials saw it, Dr. Banda had always kept a way open to remain in federation on his own terms, and even had his followers boycott the Monckton Commission so that they need not take a public stand. C.L.P. spokesmen offered various estimates of their membership to the Monckton Commission; the largest was 55,000 full members and 70,000 'recruits, who were on the party's books with a view to training for full membership'. In April 1961 their publicity secretary said they had thirty-six branches.

The party's original policy statement, issued in December 1958, offered to provide 'intellectual, realistic and benevolent leadership'. Its aim was national emancipation with 'full national status for all the inhabitants irrespective of colour, race or religion'. Holding that no effective inter-racial partnership was possible as long as Nyasaland remained in association with Southern Rhodesia, it advocated a federation with Northern Rhodesia and Tanganyika, to remain within the Commonwealth. It sought the immediate introduction of universal suffrage on a common roll with constitutional safeguards for minorities, and that 'English language shall not by any means be compulsory' (in official dealings? in the legislature?). In evidence before the Monckton Commission, Mr. T. D. T. Banda included 'tribal authorities' among the minorities to be safeguarded. He thought chiefs should have more powers and responsibilities. He also said that there should be a five-year period of transition to self-government, and that his party would consider proposals for a limited franchise during that period. He did not commit himself on the question whether Nyasaland might remain in the federation during the period of transition, nor whether federation would be more acceptable if the three territories had equal representation.

On economic problems the C.L.P. represented to the Commission that an agricultural revolution could not only make Nyasaland self-supporting but enable it to supply all central and southern Africa.

Foreign investment would be welcomed for the development of natural resources which had been neglected (water, water power and minerals) and skills which had been suppressed (notably metal working). The party also thought a new railway should be built to give a shorter haul from Nyasaland to the Portuguese coast.

Although at the outset none of the leading members of Congress joined the C.L.P.—since they had acquiesced in the expulsion of T. D. T. Banda—its existence offered an alternative allegiance to those who were dissatisfied either with the militant policy adopted after Dr. Banda's return or with his conduct of party affairs. The three older members of the Legislative Council, Messrs. Chinyama, Chijozi and Kwenje, at first dissociated themselves from unconstitutional action without leaving Congress, but after the emergency was over they left the Malawi Party and joined the C.L.P. Mr. Wellington Chirwa had joined it earlier, while the state of emergency was in force.

The formation of the Christian Democratic Party was announced in October 1960 by Mr. Chester Katsonga. Like the Congress Liberation Party it professed aims identical with those of Malawi but proposed to pursue these by Christian (i.e. non-violent) means. Mr. Katsonga had been a student in a Catholic seminary and his movement was said to have the blessing, if not the more substantial support, of the Catholic Archbishop. The issue of *Malawi News* which followed his announcement was devoted entirely to an exposure of the plans of the Catholic Church for world domination, of which this was taken as an instance. Mr. Katsonga, however, asserted that all the help he had had from the Archbishop was the loan of a typewriter.

The Christian Democratic Party, like the Congress Liberation Party, in its few months as an independent organization advocated the pursuit of political aims by constitutional methods. It explained that the word 'Christian' was used because resort to violence is un-Christian, but the party was open to adherents of any religion or sect. Its grounds of opposition to Malawi, apart from its leader's personal grievance, were three: Dr. Banda had not in fact extricated Nyasaland from the Federation, but had implicitly accepted federation in accepting the Lancaster House agreement, Malawi pursued its aims by intimidating its opponents, and it planned to exterminate both the Dutch Reformed and the Catholic churches and set up a 'national church'.

The party's statement of aims is reproduced in Appendix II.

Mr. Katsonga's grievance was that he had spent large sums of money when he was chairman of the reception committee for Dr. Banda's return and had then been ignored by the Malawi Party; like all the other former office-holders who left it he regarded Dr. Banda as a dictator who would not listen to anyone. In January 1961 his party claimed a membership of 2,000 paying a subscription of 2s. in urban and 1s. in rural areas, and in February he made a three-day tour of the Southern Province in which he held discussions, said to be highly gratifying, with chiefs and headmen. At this time, however, he had already lost his only transport vehicle through failing to keep up instalment payments. When I made his acquaintance in February he had a two-roomed office in Blantyre where two clerks worked; the inner—'president's'—room was completely bare. He spoke of trying to raise funds in London.

There was therefore nothing surprising in the announcement in April that the two opposition parties had agreed on amalgamation with the title of Christian Liberation Party, Mr. T. D. T. Banda as Chairman and Mr. Katsonga as Vice-Chairman. They described their aims as 'to fight against all forms of violence, intimidation and communistic practices being introduced in this country through activities of the Malawi Congress Party. We are determined to eliminate all sorts of hooliganism in the field of politics'.

THE UNITED FEDERAL PARTY

The United Federal Party is the Nyasaland branch of a party which was formed by the merger in 1957 of the United Rhodesia Party of Southern Rhodesia, led by Mr. Garfield Todd, and the Federal Party which grew out of the United Central Africa Association created to organize support for federation in the referendum of 1953.

In the first federal elections the four European representatives from Nyasaland were chosen on a franchise which reflected the provisions then in force for the selection of non-officials for the territorial legislature. In addition to the education and property qualifications imposed, electors had to be members of a recognized association. The Nyasaland Association was formed to encourage registration for these elections.

At the 1956 elections the Association and the Federal Party agreed on a joint list of candidates, on a programme drawn up by a Blantyre lawyer, Mr. M. V. Blackwood, which included the aim 'to protect and further the interests of Europeans in Nyasaland'. Two Federal Party branches protested that this aim was contrary to their principle of racial partnership, and two candidates, Mr. Collins and Mr. Dixon, dissociated themselves from it. In 1961 neither of these men was in the field in Nyasaland; Mr. Collins had become a Federal M.P. and Mr. Dixon had retired from politics. The two Nyasaland Association members returned in 1956 were Mr. Blackwood and Mr. Little. Their Nyasaland-first plank was thought to indicate a qualified enthusiasm for federation, but after the declaration of the emergency they appear to have concluded that this association with the Rhodesias was the best way to protect the interests of Europeans in Nyasaland, and they with the other European unofficial members joined the United Federal Party.

The party has its headquarters in Salisbury, and a separate division for each of the three territories. Its president is Sir Roy Welensky, the Prime Minister of the Federation. In March 1961 the Nyasaland party had offices at Blantyre, Limbe, Lilongwe, Cholo, Mlanje and Mzuzu. Three more had been formed by the end of April, in the Nkata Bay and Mzimba districts and at Mphasa. Since the support of a majority of European voters can be taken for granted, its efforts were concentrated on seeking African members. This, it was realized, could only be done through African organizers. It was announced that all the officers of the Mzuzu, Mphasa, Nkata Bay and Mzimba branches were African. Most of the leading African members were formerly prominent members of Congress. The first to join the U.F.P. was Mr. Mathews Phiri, a former president of Congress, who changed his allegiance on his release from detention during the emergency and in 1960 was Vice-President of the Nyasaland U.F.P. The Limbe branch was run by Mr. Mussah, the first Nyasaland trade union leader. Mr. Harry Jonga, a Blantyre trader who was prominent in a number of non-political and charitable organizations, became party organizer for the Southern Province in February 1961. Messrs. Chinyama and Chijozi announced their adherence slightly later. They explained that their earlier fears of federation had proved groundless—African land had not been taken away and colour bar restrictions, instead of being extended to Nyasaland, had been relaxed elsewhere—and that they now saw what economic benefits it had brought. In the statement announcing their new stand they said they foresaw a time when the Federal Prime Minister would be an African.[1] Mr. Chinyama was one of the elder statesmen who were hurt because Dr. Banda did not take their advice— advice (it appeared) on the internal organization of the party rather than on aims or tactics.

Malawi supporters, for whom 'he that is not with us is against us', professed to see no difference between the U.F.P. and the dissident African parties and indeed predicted that the latter would formally join the U.F.P. A U.F.P. organizer admitted that their primary aim was to secure support from Africans who were dissatisfied with Malawi for whatever reason, and straws in the wind sometimes suggested that take-over bids were being made. But there were certainly many Africans whose hostility to federation was not mitigated by their disagreements with Dr. Banda. It was widely said that most of the prominent African U.F.P. members had had some kind of assistance from the party in financial difficulties. This was denied on behalf of Chinyama and Chi-

[1] *Nyasaland Times*, 24 March.

jozi, but Dr. Banda repeatedly asserted it in public without provoking any rejoinder from the U.F.P.

In view of the state of feeling in the country the U.F.P. had to show some discretion in campaigning. Like the other parties, it had its conspicuous landrovers, and it occasionally held meetings. But it relied primarily on building up small groups where it found a nucleus of support, or dissatisfaction with Malawi—particularly where the village headman favoured it. Malawi members sometimes indicated that village headmen who opposed them would suffer when they came into power. For headmen without strong political views this posed the problem which horse to back, and some backed the U.F.P., especially in the neighbourhood of Lilongwe. As a lady organizer explained, 'Where the village headman is on our side we get support. Where he is Malawi they don't allow it.' The party also had the adherence of some people who had actually suffered injuries in the period of disturbances.

The organizers sought to spread understanding of the tangible benefits of federation and to emphasize their principle of 'merit not race' as the criterion for participation in government. The party was in a certain difficulty because it was in fact the party of European interests and was bound to champion these, apart from the fact that its leading members were temperamentally in sympathy with them. The indignant protests of its leaders at what they considered as a widening of the franchise beyond what was agreed on at Lancaster House might be gratifying to those of its African supporters who would have been qualified on the narrower interpretation, but were not calculated to win new adherents.

3. CANDIDATES

MALAWI

Spokesmen of every party at some time announced their intention of contesting every seat on both rolls, and on 5 May the correspondent of the *Nyasaland Times* stated that a contest was likely for every seat (though not necessarily a three-cornered one). An editorial in the same issue predicted that the U.F.P. would not seek to win more than about five lower roll seats and Malawi could only hope to snatch one or two seats on the higher.

Dr. Banda made a tour of the Central and Northern Provinces in February and applied to register as a voter in Kasungu, his own birthplace. But as he neither lived, worked, nor had a business there, he had to return and register in Blantyre. Mr. Sattar Sacranie visited these areas at the same time, partly to urge the Asian community to register, and at one or two centres sundowner parties were given in honour of Dr. Banda at which Mr. Sacranie pledged the support of the Asian community for him.

It was commonly believed, however, that the main object of Dr. Banda's journey was to discuss the nomination of candidates, and that while in the Northern Province he secured the agreement of the chiefs to back his nominees and discourage opposition. He had earlier stated that candidates should stand in their home districts. This principle proved impossible to apply in the case of Mr. Chiume and Mr. Orton Chirwa, who are both from Nkata Bay, and it was also disregarded in the selection of Mr. Willie Chokani for Chiradzulu. *Malawi News* repeatedly announced that only the Doctor would decide who the candidates were to be. Mr. Chisiza asserted that he would consult 'the top members', and added that he 'would not select a Matinga [the founder of the short-lived Progressive Party which accepted federation] and think that people would accept it.' But it is clear that there was no question of allowing branches to find their own candidates.

By the end of April reports were circulating in the press of dissatisfaction within the party. Members who had been passed over were alleged to have said they would stand as independents, and it was also reported that the dissatisfied members were forming a breakaway group; the latter statement was promptly denied, and nothing happened to justify it. Reports of internal dissensions were emphasized by U.F.P. supporters, but as nomination day approached there was nothing to substantiate them.

The Malawi campaign proper may be said to have been launched at a meeting in Zomba on 28 May where Dr. Banda, following the example of Nkrumah in 1954, announced the names of twenty candidates for lower roll seats and two for seats on the higher roll, at the same time reminding his audience that the authority to select them himself had been vested in him when he became Life President of the party in September 1960.

He himself, as was expected, would contest the combined constituency of Kasungu–Fort Manning, in which his birthplace is situated. Nkata Bay was allotted to Mr. Orton Chirwa, Rumpi to Mr. Chiume and Karonga to Mr. D. Chisiza. Mr. John Msonthi, who had acted as Publicity Secretary while the leading members of the party were absent at the Lancaster House conference, was to stand in Kota-Kota. The prescriptive right of Mr. Chipembere to Fort Johnston was recognized by the nomination of his father, Archdeacon Chipembere. The three Provincial Chairmen were nominated, Mr. M. Q. Y. Chibambo for Mzimba South, Mr. R. B. Chidzanja for Lilongwe Urban and Mr. Kuntumanje for Zomba. In the Southern Province the District Chairmen of Cholo and Mlanje were to contest their respective districts, and the organizing secretary for Chikwawa and Port Herald was nominated for the combined constituency. The candidate for Ncheu was N. A. Willard Gomani, the son of the Gomani who resigned his office in sympathy with the demonstrators against federation in 1953. After this event the office of Superior Native Authority was abolished, and Gomani's vassals became independent Native Authorities, but his son had not lost his status of paramount in the eyes of the Ngoni population. Of the remaining candidates, four were school teachers and two were described as business men. These last, however, failed to pass the English test. One was replaced by Mr. Somanje, the Acting Treasurer-General of the party (in Chipembere's absence), who had been a foundation member of the Nyasaland African Congress and of the Ndirande Club, a welfare organization which built its own community centre outside Blantyre some years before government policy was concerned with services of this kind. The second, who was district chairman in Cholo, was replaced by his district secretary. When the team was finally made up, it included ten party officials, four from the central executive and six from the branches. Four Malawi candidates were university graduates, as were four of the independents to be described later; the U.F.P. had one, the C.L.P. did not muster any.

Two Malawi candidates stood for higher roll seats, Mr. I. K. Surtee, the president of the Coloured community, for the Central Province and Mr. Mikeka Mkandawire, the manager of a bar in Soche and founder and secretary of the African Chamber of Commerce, for the Northern Province. The latter had been Rumpi's favourite son, and was compensated in this way when the Rumpi seat was allotted to Chiume. Some commentators thought he would find himself ill-placed to solicit votes in the area where he had been active before the emergency, and that this was a poor substitute for a safe seat. Another view was that the outcome would depend on which of the two candidates alienated more voters. Both these constituencies had a large missionary vote, which was believed to be hostile to the U.F.P.

THE U.F.P.

The parts of the U.F.P. constitution which concern the selection of candidates are modelled on similar rules in the United Kingdom, and the party emphasized their democratic nature in contrast to Malawi methods. Headquarters maintains a panel of candidates to which names can be added at any time on the nomination of branches. When an election is imminent each branch selects its candidates at a meeting of members, where names may be proposed from the floor. The choice is made after a three-minute speech by each aspirant.

It was admitted that in choosing lower roll candidates branches had to rely on the headquarters panel, but it was emphatically stated that in no case were the wishes of branches overruled.

The problems of a party organized in this way and dedicated to partnership (however defined) were considerable. Obviously the ethnic affiliations of candidates were relevant both to their chances of selection by branches and to their prospects of winning votes. Some observers had expected the policy of partnership to be symbolized by finding a higher roll constituency for the African vice-president, but, whatever other reasons there might have been against this, it was probably thought that many Europeans would be unwilling to vote for an African.

The party did in fact put up one non-European candidate for the higher roll, in the one constituency, Soche, which had a non-European majority. This was Mr. Roopsingh, an Indian born in Durban, who was a member of the Nyasaland Chamber of Commerce and Blantyre Town Council. Some years earlier he had left the employment of a firm whose management had openly shown sympathy for Malawi, so that he could be represented as a victim of his political convictions. During the Lancaster House conference he had collected signatures for a telegram to Mr. Macleod asserting that the Asian delegates, in declining to ask for special protection for the Asian population, were not really representative of the opinion of their community. He had supported the proposals of the Nyasaland Chamber of Commerce for the licensing regulations which were obnoxious to Asian wholesalers; he himself had an agency business. He was said by other Asians to prefer associating with Europeans; in retaliation they cast doubt on the purity of his Asian descent. Some Europeans feared that he would lose a part of the European vote simply because his opponent was a European.

There was nothing particularly remarkable about the list of candidates for the other constituencies. Four former M.L.C's stood again: Mr. Blackwood, the leader of the unofficials in the previous legislature and now the leader of the Nyasaland division of the U.F.P. (Blantyre); Mr. Little, a business man (Limbe); Colonel Hunt, a retired Indian Army officer farming near Lilongwe (Northern Province); and Mr. Peterkins, an old resident who had a tung and tobacco farm in Cholo (Southern Districts). The contributions of the last-named to debate had been of a nature to encourage hilarity rather than rational discussion; but it is not likely that many of his constituents had read them. Mr. Blackwood had had to contest his seat in 1956, but none of the others had had this experience; all three were alleged by those who hoped to win votes from them to have paid little attention to their constituents. The candidate for Lilongwe Town was Mr. R. G. Morgan, a building and electrical contractor and chairman of the Town Council, and Mr. Leslie Sawyer, the chairman of the Lilongwe branch of the party and a quarry owner, contested the Central Districts. Mr. R. Duncan, who with his father managed a farm near Zomba, was the candidate for Shire North. Mr. Duncan's parents were old residents, well known and respected, and his prestige as a candidate derived largely from his membership of the family. The U.F.P. emphasized their candidates' service with the armed forces; they did not publicize Mr. Blackwood's university degree.

In the lower roll constituencies the U.F.P. admitted to an agreement with the C.L.P., which fell short of an election pact but had the effect of limiting the number of three-cornered fights. Malawi ascribed this to the difficulty which both parties had in finding candidates. Four constituencies were contested by both parties, Blantyre Urban, Blantyre Rural, Cholo and the Lower River. In a fifth, Chiradzulu, the U.F.P. candidate, Mr. Harry Jonga, who had joined the party with some publicity in February, resigned with equal publicity, asserting that it treated Africans 'as horses' (an allusion to the definition of partnership, ascribed to Lord Malvern, as the relationship between horse and rider). Some said he had worked as a U.F.P. organizer for as long as was necessary to pay off the debts he had incurred in running his store in Soche. He told me that he had been influenced by a visit to his wife's relatives in Southern Rhodesia, where he learnt what rural life was like under the Native Land Husbandry Act; and also that there were no Africans in the party headquarters in Salisbury.

The U.F.P. candidates included the former M.L.C's Chijozi and Chinyama, the former federal M. P. Kumbikano, their vice-chairman Mathews Phiri and three of their African organizers. One of these, Mr. Makamo, was among the first African members of the party. During the disturbances his store in Lilongwe was looted, and he took refuge in the police lines. He was admired in the party for his courage in reporting cases of intimidation, and at the time of the elections there were eleven persons serving sentences for such acts against him. He also had the rare distinction for one not a member of Malawi of having himself been convicted of threatening a political opponent (with a gun). His own methods were said to be unusually aggressive. The remaining five included the works supervisor to the Cholo District Council, a retired police sergeant, a retired hospital assistant, a former clerk in the Land Registry, and an employee of the Federal Information Department.

The descriptions of their candidates that were issued from the party headquarters made a point where possible of the area of land farmed by

D

each, implying that they were responsible citizens with a stake in the country. It has been common for retired African government servants to put their savings into farming, and the main significance of the number of farmers on the U.F.P. list is as an indication of the older average age of their candidates.

A mild sensation was caused by the original selection of a candidate to oppose Dr. Banda in Kasungu. At a branch meeting of some 250 people, the name of an English lady was proposed from the floor and secured an overwhelming majority over the two Africans whose names were before the meeting. This was Mrs. Lyster, a former teacher who had farmed with her husband in various parts of the Federation and was an active church worker and keenly interested in African welfare, though she did not speak Cinyanja. It was believed in the U.F.P. that she had secured the nomination by the emphasis on religion in her three-minute speech. To the present writer it seemed possible that members thought the cost of opposing Dr. Banda, whatever this might prove to be, could be better borne by a European. Mrs. Lyster sincerely believed that the leadership of Dr. Banda was a disaster from which the Africans must be saved. Unfortunately for her she had been involved in the bankruptcy of her husband in Southern Rhodesia, and there was no time to establish before nomination day that she was not disqualified as a candidate. It was then announced that she would be replaced by Mr. Wedson Chima, a 28-year-old clerk. On nomination day, however, Mr. Chima did not appear; he had been unable, or said he was unable, to obtain the necessary signatures for his nomination paper. The U.F.P. branch chairman, who appears to have been unaware that the names of a candidate's supporters have to be made public, complained to the press[1] that his supporters were deterred from signing by threats that their names would be made known. It appeared later that Mr. Chima was not in fact a registered voter, and this was also the case with another U.F.P. candidate.

THE C.L.P.

The C.L.P. put up seven candidates. The president, Mr. T. D. T. Banda, stood in Nkata Bay, his home district. He was said to rely on the voters in twenty-seven related villages who were divided by a long-standing enmity from the kinsmen and followers of Mr. Orton Chirwa.[2]

[1] *Rhodesia Herald*, 24 July 1961.

[2] It is assumed in some quarters that any social anthropologist who makes an election study should concentrate on this kind of 'micropolitics'. This could only be done by a prolonged stay in the locality concerned to the exclusion of the rest of the country. I make no apology for disregarding a situation which it was clear would not affect the outcome of the contest.

When interviewed he seemed to dislike the idea that a candidate or party should have stronger support in some localities than in others and assured me that he had followers everywhere.

Mr. Katsonga contested Blantyre Urban in a three-cornered fight against Mr. Augustine Bwanausi, one of the Malawi intellectuals, and Mr. Mussah, the U.F.P. organizer for Limbe. For Blantyre Rural Mr. Kwenje, the only former elected M.L.C. to stand for re-election without joining the U.F.P., opposed Mr. Andrew Mponda (U.F.P.) and Mr. Somanje, Malawi's second choice when the district organizer failed to pass the English test. In the Lower River constituency Mr. Gill Phiri, the manager of a typing agency, opposed Mr. H. M. Thompson (U.F.P.) and Mr. Chakumba for Malawi. On the Cholo candidate, Mr. G. C. Namangwiyo, no information is available. Mr. Gilbert Pondeponde, the original secretary of Mr. Katsonga's party, stood in Mlanje. He was a former detainee who, like Mr. Katsonga, had resigned from Malawi because it did not respect democratic principles. Mr. Makunami, who opposed Mr. Willie Chokani in Chiradzulu, had been a headmaster there for fifteen years and was also a village headman. He was thought to have a slightly better chance than the rest of his party because Mr. Chokani, who was an outsider to the district, had been chosen in preference to the local Malawi secretary; a good many voters accepted him as the representative of Kamuzu, but there was a noticeable lack of efficiency in the practical arrangements for which the branch secretary was responsible.

THE INDEPENDENTS

Malawi were anxious that if possible every higher roll seat should be contested, if only to register opposition to the U.F.P., and this view was shared by some of the younger Europeans who thought that the elections should give an opportunity everywhere for the expression of such liberal sentiments as might be found to exist. The six higher roll seats for which there were not Malawi candidates were contested by independents. Four of these, three Europeans and an Asian, had the endorsement of Dr. Banda. The other two, both women, stood without his blessing. None received any financial support from Malawi (or from any source). Of the five Europeans, three were closely associated with the Church of Central Africa Presbyterian (C.C.A.P.), which was founded when the European congregation of the Church of Scotland dissociated themselves from the missionaries and the African congregation. Only one of the five had been more than ten years in the country. Thus they could not hope to appeal to that section of opinion which 'knew the African' in virtue of many years' residence, interpreted the 1959 disturbances as a manifestation of his essential savagery, refused to believe that Dr. Banda would ever co-operate with Europeans, and had found an explanation of the attitude of the Scottish missionaries at the time of the emergency in their supposed Communist sympathies. They could, however, count on the support of the small number of African voters, of the Asians if they followed the lead of the Asian Convention, and, they hoped, of some Europeans who either had heeded the wind of change or were dissatisfied with their U.F.P. representatives. Members of the latter category were hard to identify. The liberal element was believed to be in the civil service, but there was no particular reason to look for it in the technical departments; the administrative officers, whose calling obliged them to think about the political situation, were a minority of the whole.

Even before the end of the emergency it had been argued in conversations between Dr. Banda and his European friends that it would be advisable for Europeans to contest the higher roll seats and that those who did need not commit themselves to membership of Malawi. The endorsement of the party, which carried with it that of the Asian Convention, was naturally of most value where there was a high proportion of non-European voters. To rank and file Malawi members it was no more than a device to avoid the odium of the party name, and it was interpreted as such by the U.F.P. The fact that the most active of the independent candidates were in close touch with Dr. Banda seemed to lend colour to this interpretation.

However, the reality was not so simple. The independents, though *ex hypothesi* opposed to the U.F.P., and in some cases on terms of close friendship with Malawi leaders, preferred not to be committed to unconditional support of Dr. Banda in details of policy. One of them indeed was not very sympathetic to Malawi and regarded the independent position as one from which possible excesses could be checked by people not committed to opposition on all points. The others saw their role as that of friendly and constructive critics. While some thought it more likely that they would act as a restraint on precipitate action, others expected to form a ginger group if victory should make the party complacent. All believed that the appearance of a number of Europeans with whom Dr. Banda was prepared to co-operate was an earnest of his sincere desire to seek friendship with the immigrant communities.

On the day after nomination day all six held a press conference. This was not prepared in advance, except that a statement was drawn up and signed by all six to the effect that they had two principles in common: Nyasaland must be a non-racial society (as opposed to a multi-racial partnership) and any association with external territories must be freely negotiated by a popularly chosen government.

The most active among the independents was Mr. Colin Cameron, who contested Soche. Mr. Cameron was a young lawyer who had come to the country shortly before the return of Dr. Banda. During the emergency he had been responsible for the provision of legal aid for detainees and had defended many of them himself, and he had been in the close councils of the founders of the new Malawi Party. He had also a considerable Asian clientele through whom he was personally known among the Asian community. It was thought that some Europeans might vote for him in preference to an Asian, though this factor was not present when he decided to stand. The European voters in this constituency included a small number of missionaries and civil servants, but were mainly business men and their employees.

Altogether there were 360 Asian, 300 European and 100 African voters. The issue here depended directly on the Asian vote: if the members of the Convention followed the lead of their president, the result could not be in doubt. A U.F.P. victory would be a vote of no confidence in Mr. Sacranie and a declaration of Asian hostility to Malawi.

In the Shire North constituency (Zomba with Kasupe and Fort Johnston) there were 522 voters, 84 Africans, 50 Asians, 3 Coloured and the rest European. Of the last category only 48 were permanent residents, most of them farmers, who could be assumed to support the U.F.P. The rest were civil servants, whose choice was thought likely to be influenced by their expectations of their future under the type of responsible government envisaged by Malawi and the U.F.P. respectively. This again might vary with their seniority, and with such prejudices as might be characteristic of different social backgrounds. An important distinction was that between the employees of the federalized services, many of whom had come from Rhodesia, and those of the territorial departments. Many were believed to be unfavourably disposed towards Mr. Blackwood because of the changes in their conditions of service which he had secured from the previous legislature. Thirteen missionaries could be counted on not to support the U.F.P., but their attitude to a Malawi-backed candidate was in doubt.

The candidate who secured Dr. Banda's endorsement for this seat was Major Peter Moxon, who had settled in Nyasaland after serving with a Nyasa regiment in the second world war. Major Moxon had a farm near Zomba and a bar in Balaka, the other major centre of population in his constituency. He also managed a luncheon centre in Zomba which was frequented by African civil servants. Like his U.F.P. opponent, he had been divorced and remarried. In Major Moxon's case this event was a good deal further in the past; on the other hand, he had been divorced by an Englishwoman and married an African. His leisure time was spent more in the company of Africans than of Europeans and he had few close contacts in Zomba social circles. Nevertheless he had lost the Zomba seat by only ten votes in a bye-election in 1959.

In Blantyre Mr. Blackwood was opposed by the Reverend Andrew Ross of the C.C.A.P., who had preached sermons in Zomba which moved the more conservative members of the congregation to walk out of the church, had kept in close touch with detainees during the emergency and had had his full share of the odium that attached at that time to any European who was sympathetic to Congress. This constituency had the highest proportion of European voters, and the highest, after Zomba, of civil servants. These included the staffs of the federal departments with headquarters in Blantyre, notably commerce, immigration, health and non-African education, all of whom might be expected to vote for the maintenance of federation. Mr. Ross's friends were mostly among the younger Europeans, some of whom he had met on the football field, while he shared with others a common Scottish background. His status as a minister was probably a liability rather than an asset. Many people, including his colleague the Reverend Andrew Doig, held that religion should be kept apart from political contests.

Mr. Bheda, the Asian independent with Malawi backing, contested Lilongwe Town. He was chairman of the finance committee of the Town Council, of which his U.F.P. opponent was chairman. He was not very impressive as a speaker, and relied principally on the committed vote of loyal members of the Asian Convention.

In the week before nomination day Malawi headquarters reported that they were receiving telephone calls from people who wanted to know if there was to be no contest in Limbe. This inspired a last-minute search for independents to contest the two remaining higher roll seats, Limbe and the Southern Districts. After dramatic negotiations two were found, both women.

In the Southern Districts Mr. Peterkins was opposed by Mrs. Katharine Robertson, a doctor and the wife of a missionary of the C.C.A.P. at Mlanje, in the centre of the tea-growing area. Mrs. Robertson had succeeded in breaking down some of the antagonism to the mission which reached its height after the revelation of the supposed massacre plot, and had persuaded some of the younger women that the panic measures of protection recommended by the planting community were exaggerated. She and her husband had more European friends than many missionaries. Her constituents were mainly the managers and employees of tea estates. The chief concentration was in the districts of Cholo and Mlanje; but even here a canvassing round might consist in driving forty miles to see four voters and finding that two of them were not at home. In Chikwawa and Port Herald there was a small number of civil servants, Asian traders and employees of the Agricultural Production and Marketing Board.

The independent candidate for Limbe was Mrs. Ruxton, a Cambridge graduate and the wife of an engineer. Her initial support came from a small number of Europeans who during the emergency had felt that there should be some opposition to the U.F.P. and had formed a branch of Mr. Garfield Todd's Central African Party. Though she shared with the other independents the conviction that only a policy of co-operation with Malawi had any prospect of success and that the strength of the opposition to federation was irresistible, and hoped to win the votes of Europeans who had come round to this view, she was personally not very sympathetic to Malawi and had defended the government's emergency policy in a letter to a church newspaper in the United Kingdom. She also held that any connection with Malawi was still a fatal disadvantage to a candidate in a predominantly European electorate, and preferred not to have Dr. Banda's endorsement.

Her constituency included 600 European voters, 100 Asians, 23 'Mauritians' (i.e. Goans) and about a dozen Africans. Of these 600 were concentrated in Limbe township, including the two great blocks of employees of the Imperial Tobacco Company and the Nyasaland Railways. The railways were believed to have less enthusiasm for the U.F.P. than the I.T.C., which was regarded as solidly for it. The hundred voters outside Limbe were scattered in inaccessible places.

All the three U.F.P. candidates who were members of the previous legislature had won their seats without serious campaigning, and all were said to have failed to keep in touch with their constituents and thus incurred a certain amount of unpopularity from which their opponents might profit. But against this had to be set the conviction of large numbers of Europeans that only the U.F.P. could protect their interests and that it would effectively do so.

In these two constituencies the independent candidates needed a high Asian and a low European poll. Those Asians who voted could be counted on to support the independents, and most Europeans who went to the polls would probably vote U.F.P. But in addition to the normal proportion of people too indifferent to vote there was believed to be an unknown number of Europeans who no longer wished to vote for the U.F.P. but could not bring themselves to vote against it.

To these six independents there was added another whose principal function was to promote a three-cornered contest. This was Mr. E. M. Mtawali, who stood for Shire North. He was a former medical assistant who had taken an active part in a community development scheme in his home village. He had been a nominated member of the previous legislature, had been appointed to the Executive Council with a special attachment to the local government and social services division, and had served on the committee on localization of the civil service. Mr. Mtawali was one of the best speakers in the Legislative Council, and his experience of the Executive Council gave him an advantage over every other African candidate and all the other independents. Some civil servants, however, thought his talents were for the execution rather than the framing of policy. He was believed to have been urged to stand by some senior civil servants, notably the Secretary for Local Government and Social Services, Mr. Ingham. *Malawi News*[1] made this assertion with the comment that Mr. Ingham was nearly the most unpopular with Africans of all high government officials. Some weeks later, Mr. Ingham wrote to the paper, 'At no time have I suggested to Mr. Mtawali that he should stand as a candidate in the forthcoming elections nor have I in any way whatsoever supported his candidature'. The paper commented, 'It should now be clear to the public that Mr. Ingham does not support Mr. Mtawali'.[2]

Mr. Mtawali had never been divorced, a fact that guaranteed him a proportion of the women's vote. He was generally respected, and his candidature was calculated to appeal to those voters for whom an election was a matter of choosing an individual representative for his personal worth. Indeed this was how he saw it himself. He considered, as he said in his manifesto, that his combination of familiarity with village problems and attitudes and experience of the practical implications of government policies gave him something to offer the voters. But when it was suggested that he might contest one of the other seats for which no independent had been found, he indicated that he was not interested in a forlorn hope. Observers expected his support to come from voters who, while they regarded secession as inevitable and so would not support the U.F.P., had misgivings about Dr. Banda's hold over his militant Youth League members and were afraid that a Malawi victory would be followed by new disturbances; and also from some Catholics who had been alarmed when *Malawi News* published its denunciation of their church.

He himself stated that he was 'not against Dr. Banda'. He had never spoken in favour of federation and had never been included in the list of 'stooges' who were ritually denounced at Malawi meetings; it was said that Dr. Banda wanted to give him important administrative responsibilities. But Malawi supporters feared that he would prejudice all chances of co-operation with Dr. Banda by opposing the candidate who had his endorsement.

[1] 20 July 1961.
[2] *Malawi News*, 10 August 1961.

4. Programmes and Manifestos

In this election there was very little difference in the programmes of the various parties. Although the U.F.P. maintained that it was not legally possible for Nyasaland to leave the Federation, this was in fact the major question which divided them from the others, and to a large extent the aims of internal policy were the same for all. Indeed one sometimes noticed that points originally raised by independents appeared as part of U.F.P. policy; even the word 'non-racial', used by the independents to signify their alternative to partnership as understood by the U.F.P., was heard subsequently on the lips of U.F.P. candidates.

The attitude to federation was, then, the crucial point of difference. The U.F.P. maintained that Nyasaland should remain within the federation and become self-governing (i.e. no longer responsible to the Colonial Office) in all territorial functions, with increasing African participation by defined stages. 'As Federation advances towards independence adequate arrangements should be made to ensure that all peoples are just as well protected as before.'

Malawi's manifesto did not mention the subject except incidentally, when stating that the party, 'as part of its uncompromising stand against the imposed Central African Federation', would 'work to take over health services'. Party headquarters explained that the end of federation could be taken for granted, and were surprised that this sentence could be read to imply its continuance.

The C.L.P. proposed to 'create conditions whereby constitutional measures could be made for the return of all departments now under the Federal Government back to the Territorial Government'. Future arrangements for association with other countries should be made 'by means of negotiation and agreement and NOT by force or Race Supremacy'.

Among the independents Major Moxon and Mrs. Ruxton agreed that some association between Nyasaland and neighbouring territories was in its interest, but insisted, as did all those who took part in the press conference, that whatever associations might be created or maintained must have the consent of the electorate. The group who held the conference agreed that the proper place for discussion of this question was the Federal Review Conference. Mr. Cameron elaborated on the theme of African opposition; in his view, with which Mrs. Ruxton concurred, 'there could be no political stability' as long as federation was imposed against the will of the electorate. He gave reasons: the impending domestic crisis in Southern Rhodesia which was bound to result from that country's racial policy should not be allowed to hold back the progress of Nyasaland, and the principle of 'Partnership' as practised in the Federation had meant no more than 'a means of extending the period of white domination by removing (and publicizing greatly) small instances of the colour bar and creating an *élite* class of Africans for absorption into the European Community, who are then ostracized by their fellow Africans'. Mr. Bheda said: 'Here we do not want a federation for the sake of Southern Rhodesia. I believe that a federation acceptable to the people of this country must be, as it ought to be, for the sake of Nyasaland.' Mr. Mtawali did not discuss this question.

The U.F.P. disposed of the existence of nationalist feeling by proposing that 'everyone should be taught a sense of nationhood both of Nyasaland and of the Federation'. Malawi naturally took their own nationhood for granted. The independents recognized it as an irresistible force; some welcomed it; all were convinced that co-operation with it was the only realistic course.

Education figured very prominently in the Malawi programme, rather less so in the others. Malawi proposed to aim at universal education, to take immediate steps to see that all children who entered primary schools should complete the course, to provide increased opportunities for secondary education, including the grant of bursaries, and to take immediate steps to increase facilities for secondary education for girls. Domestic training would also be provided. The party proposed to expand technical and commercial education and would encourage workers to raise their standard of competence by taking evening classes and correspondence courses. A mass literacy drive was envisaged. Higher education was seen primarily as a qualification for African civil servants; all available scholarships and bursaries would be taken up, but as soon as possible a university would be opened at Khondowe (Livingstonia).

In the view of the U.F.P. all African children should be educated up to Standard VI and no child meriting further education should be deprived of the opportunity. Overseas scholarships should be provided 'with the particular purpose of training Africans to take up important posts' within Nyasaland. Special attention should be given to the education of women and girls, and also to technical and vocational training. All education should emphasize the need to increase productivity and a sense of responsibility.

The Christian Liberation Party would 'press for the creation of adequate educational facilities for all races' and held that this could be done by giving all races adequate representation on statutory bodies concerned with the subject.

Mr. Cameron, followed closely by Mr. Bheda, and not quite so closely by Major Moxon and Mrs. Robertson, urged that priority should be given to secondary education, and that state secondary schools should be racially integrated, without prejudice to the right of any parents to pay for the education of their children in schools of their own choosing. Other branches of education to be developed were an agricultural college and farm institutes, night schools for technical and commercial training and broadcast education for adults on the lines adopted in India. In primary schools Standard VIII should be the minimum requirement for teachers, and local authorities should be made responsible for them. Mr. Cameron favoured a liberal arts college as the first step towards a university at Livingstonia. Mr. Mtawali said, 'We should put more emphasis on secondary and technical education', but included in his list of key points 'the encouragement of education in all its forms'. Mrs. Ruxton gave priority to primary education, suggesting that schools should be built by community development schemes. She emphasized the importance of agricultural and industrial efficiency; to proposals for training institutions and courses she added the creation of a branch of the Labour Department to be concerned with time and motion studies, job-rating and training within industry; and the utilization of the technical assistance offered by the International Labour Office.

Social services other than education were not mentioned by the U.F.P. Malawi promised to abolish all discrimination in health services 'once and for all'. It would endeavour to provide increased medical facilities, and would carry out a health education programme. The party would 'review the question of housing, especially in towns with a view to relieving the people of the burden of excessive rates and also to providing better houses without discrimination'. Malawi would endeavour to provide libraries and cultural centres and special facilities for the disabled.

The C.L.P. would 'press for more health demonstrators and medical orderlies' to work in the villages, and for the expansion of medical training. 'Private medical practitioners should be encouraged to stay in the country.'

Mr. Cameron would develop the existing health service under territorial control, with emphasis on the preventive side (also one of Mrs. Robertson's priorities); recruit doctors and nurses with 'emphasis on the responsibility they will have to take and difficulties to face rather than on salary and perquisites'; encourage newly qualified doctors to do their year of residence in Nyasaland; develop the training of nurses and have maternity clinics built by community development schemes.

Mrs. Ruxton did not mention health services but urged the extension of social welfare activities for which workers should be trained under the auspices of the Council for Social Services. She recommended the introduction of compulsory registration of births and deaths 'as a preliminary to a scheme of social security'. Housing for workers should be provided along the lines approved by the International Labour Organization.

The U.F.P. proposed the creation of an integrated civil service for the Federation; that 'the existing rights of Civil Servants must be preserved' (apparently a reference to persons at present serving, not to rights as such); that priority in promotion should be given to officers already serving in the Protectorate; and that the service should be open to persons of all races and advancement be on merit only. Its manifesto did not mention the acceleration in local recruitment which was already official policy.

Malawi, while believing that 'African advancement in the civil service should become one of the cardinal points of government policy', offered an assurance to the members of the existing civil service of complete security of tenure and protection from unfair discrimination. A Public Service Commission would be set up (there was actually one in being). An Institute of Public Administration would be created to train 'Africans and others' for senior posts; this was described as a more economical method than sending men abroad for training.

The C.L.P. asserted that the civil service should be localized 'without causing irritation or racial prejudice to non-African civil servants.' It stood for equal pay for equal work.

The independents in general recognized both the importance of retaining experienced civil servants and the need to increase local recruitment. Mr. Cameron based his argument on the high cost of expatriate personnel. Mr. Bheda would welcome any suggestions 'aimed at securing for this country the services and ability of people trained in the art of administration'. Mr. Mtawali believed in rapid localization but recognized 'the need to retain the special services of expatriate officers for some time to come'.

Major Moxon declared his support for the policy recommended by the Adu report[1] on localization, adding that generous compensation must be offered to expatriate officers wishing to leave Nyasaland and 'equally realistic inducements for men of ability to stay'. His manifesto did not mention the United Kingdom White Paper on 'Service with Overseas Governments',[2] though this had appeared some months before and was naturally a topic of interest among the senior civil servants of his constituency.

All parties considered the position of Native Authorities and village headmen. The U.F.P. offered them substantially increased salaries and

[1] Localization Committee Report, Nyasaland Protectorate, 1960.
[2] Cmnd. 1193, 1960.

increased responsibility; it considered that adequate finance should be provided for District Councils. Malawi held that 'the traditional practical [*sic*: perhaps "political"] institutions must be reconciled with the new parliamentary structure at the centre so that modern democratic government can be established'. The C.L.P. 'would be in duty bound to work hand in hand with the chiefs', and held that when District Councils became elective the chiefs should be *ex officio* members. Malawi on the other hand proposed to set up representative local authorities on the United Kingdom model, in which the chiefs would only be formal chairmen. Local authority treasuries should be made more efficient.

Malawi also proposed that township authorities should be made wholly elective, a matter which was not considered in any other manifesto, but which was topical because the representation of Africans by nomination had just been introduced in the Blantyre-Limbe municipality.

The main points of U.F.P. economic policy were that 'there should be encouragement in every way of a financial, agricultural and commercial structure which will conduce to the maximum possible employment'; 'there should be established markets at adequate prices for the growers of foodstuffs'; and tourism should be encouraged. A matter of special interest to Asian voters was recent Nyasaland legislation on trading licences, which, by increasing the fees paid by owners of business premises, placed them at a disadvantage relatively to the travelling salesmen of wholesale firms in Southern Rhodesia and threatened to reduce the Asian wholesalers in Nyasaland from the status of merchants to that of trading agents. On this point U.F.P. policy was 'that trading licences should not place traders at a disadvantage in relation to other traders in the Federation'.

Malawi's economic policy was expounded at great length and summed up under the three heads, 'Commercialization and modernization of agriculture, building basic economic institutions (economic infra-structure) for the economy, and training administrators and technicians'. It proposed to raise living standards, to multiply economic opportunities by, *inter alia*, 'the provision of paid employment to rural populations during the off seasons' and 'the promotion of small scale and handicraft industries'; to promote 'business activities among the less privileged'; to calculate the benefits of new economic activities in terms of social gain; to maintain stable prices and enforce better conditions of work. It would provide social security for the aged, infirm and disabled and would encourage co-operative activities. It would also provide cheap power, cheap transport and an adequate water supply.

The C.L.P. believed that 'once our rivers are harnessed to turn machinery, valleys opened up and the soil productively treated, Nyasaland will sooner or later escape the sting of hunger and poverty'. It considered that 'the time has come for setting up maize, cotton, sugar and groundnut processing plants', and would invite the Colonial Development Corporation or private investors to finance a fishing and fish-canning industry. Master Farmers[1] should be 'encouraged'.

The Malawi-backed independents concentrated their economic proposals on specific development schemes for which it was expected that external capital would be forthcoming once there was confidence in the stability of Nyasaland. Mr. Cameron and Mr. Bheda proposed a five-year plan to be drawn up after surveys by experts from the United Nations and World Bank. They made specific proposals for the irrigation of the Elephant Marsh for sugar cultivation, the extension of cotton growing and introduction of cocoa, rubber and Spanish onions; peasant cultivation of tea to supplement estate cultivation; and the recall of Mr. Sholto Douglas to study the prospects of peasant production of essential oils.[2] They proposed the introduction of processing industries, in particular a sugar refinery, a textile mill and fish and fruit canning, to be spread throughout the country and not concentrated in Limbe. Tourism should be encouraged and roads and airstrips planned to make tourist resorts more accessible. Mr. Cameron's manifesto had a special section on transport advocating the development of feeder roads 'wherever a district can show that such expenditure would be justified by the savings that improved communications would make to the existing or growing markets there'. Nyasaland labour should be employed rather than expensive machinery; if wages were adequate this would discourage emigration. The improvement of communications with Tanganyika should be discussed with the government of that country.

Major Moxon added to the list of developments a beef-raising industry, a brewery and a distillery.

Mrs. Ruxton favoured 'soliciting the nations of the free world for economic assistance to Nyasaland over a period of years', mentioned the Shire Valley Hydro-electric Scheme and the encouragement of industries to produce clothing and farm implements, and also referred to the need for control of prices. Her manifesto had a section on wage-fixing, designed to appeal to the personnel of the industrial concerns

[1] See p. 11.

[2] Mr. Sholto Douglas, an expert on this subject, had been making investigations in Nyasaland at the end of 1960 when he was declared a prohibited immigrant by the Federal Government. Mr. Douglas had not engaged in political activities, and it was generally supposed that this action—no explanation of which need legally be given—was due to his being married to an African.

which were concentrated in her constituency. She proposed the creation of a statistical office responsible for calculating the cost of living as a basis for minimum wage determinations 'with progressive increases as productivity improves', on the lines already adopted in Kenya. Mr. Mtawali stood for the encouragement of economically productive agriculture and of private capital investment. 'It would be my aim,' he wrote, 'to encourage the creation of an atmosphere which would give confidence to investors.' Mrs. Robertson emphasized the importance of the tea industry, the major economic interest in her constituency, of peasant agriculture and cottage industries, and of light industries decentralized from the Blantyre-Limbe area.

The technical inadequacy of African farming methods in Nyasaland is recognized by all non-Africans and some Africans. Attempts to enforce soil conservation rules had been resisted in Nyasaland as elsewhere in East Africa, and indeed to some rural Africans were the epitome of the oppression from which Dr. Banda was to save them. To the U.F.P. resistance to these rules was an example of the disastrous nature of Malawi leadership. But their manifesto offered no policy for this problem.

Malawi asserted that Nyasaland must modernize its agriculture and adopt better farming methods. The C.L.P. reference to Master Farmers (who attain that status by following official instructions) could be taken as its contribution on the subject.

Major Moxon, counting on the release of new energies under nationalist leadership, wrote, 'I foresee, and if elected will do all in my power to foster an agricultural revolution. . . . I would like to see the emergence of a class of yeoman farmers.' Mr. Cameron and Mr. Bheda urged that the Minister for Agriculture who would be responsible for promoting new methods must be an African.

Another thorny subject which was approached only obliquely was that of land rights. Although this had not become a central political issue as it did in Kenya, there was considerable feeling among Africans that undeveloped land on alienated estates should be thrown open for settlement, and for some years demands had been made that the land acquired by missions should be surrendered. The U.F.P. stand on this was explicit—'the land rights of all peoples in the territory should be guaranteed'. Malawi did not mention it. The C.L.P. undertook to 'disallow any legislation intended to repossess land or property legally owned by any individual person, church or corporate body. . . . The present Land Tenure may continue provided it was not intended to deprive the people concerned of their land rights.' Mr. Mtawali wrote, 'I see no reason to interfere with land title in cases where the occupier is actively engaged in contributing to the national economy.' The other independents did not mention the question; one of them appeared to bear of it for the first time when African voters raised it during a canvass.

The control of immigration, a subject which was equally thorny for Asians, was ignored by Malawi, and the U.F.P. manifesto had nothing to say on the wider subject of the admission of Indians into the Federation. Among a list of aims concerned with the implementation of partnership, however, it included 'freedom of movement of all persons of good character within the Federation subject to the land rights of the peoples of the respective Territories'. This had some bearing on the existing restrictions on movement between the three territories. The C.L.P. advocated selective immigration of British subjects and others who 'specialized in certain trades and skills' as long as their technical knowledge was needed. Mr. Cameron was for the removal of 'the present petty and inhuman regulations' and of the stigma imposed on certain persons by declaring them prohibited immigrants. Mrs. Ruxton would 'control the further entry to this country of aliens seeking employment which can well be done by nationals'.

The U.F.P. list of aims under the heading 'Partnership' included the principle that 'all remaining vestiges of unfair discrimination' should be removed. In the Cinyanja version of the manifesto which appeared in the *Nyasaland Forum*[1] in the week before polling day this was rendered by a phrase which meant literally 'that bad customs concerned with choice be thrown away'. They explained that the Native Land Trust Act, protecting African rights, was an example of racial discrimination which was not unfair. All races were to be given 'the opportunity of security of land tenure'.

A cardinal point in the U.F.P. programme was the transference of non-African agriculture to federal control. This apparently innocuous proposal was believed by Africans to open the door to some invasion of their land rights. But since all other candidates were opposed to the continuance of the federation in its existing form, if at all, they did not argue this point.

Only Malawi offered a foreign policy, one of 'discretional alignment and neutralism'. The party would seek solidarity with other African states and give moral and material support to 'our brethren who are still languishing under the full force of foreign domination'. It would also cultivate 'the habit of lending assistance to needy brothers however meagre our resources may be'.

Malawi's manifesto had a section on the independence of the judiciary which, apart from the proposal to create a Judicial Services Commission, simply described the existing constitutional position.

[1] 8 August.

The C.L.P. manifesto opened with a vague statement about respect for 'all religious bodies'. Only the C.L.P. expressly mentioned trade unions, though Mrs. Ruxton gave her support to the principle of collective bargaining. The C.L.P. favoured 'healthy trade unions which should remain and operate away from political organizations'. Only the C.L.P. mentioned the military and police, in a curious statement concluding that 'for the sake of maintaining Law and Order experienced personnel are required'.

Points peculiar to Mr. Cameron's manifesto were his explicit assertion that immigrants should have no rights which were not possessed by the indigenous people, his express denunciation of *apartheid*, and the suggestion that the executive bodies of youth organizations should be 'representative of the parents of the boys and girls who are in them'. This last point envisaged particularly the Boy Scouts with wholly European management and, in his constituency, a largely Asian membership.

Only Major Moxon expressly criticized the U.F.P., remarking that they had consistently condemned African nationalism, were suspected by Africans and could not be expected to co-operate effectively with them since they were bound by policies which 'must primarily meet the needs of another country'.

Most party candidates did not issue individual manifestos. But Mr. Makunami, the C.L.P. candidate for Chiradzulu, himself a village headman and recently retired after forty years as a teacher, offered to secure improvements in conditions for both teachers and village headmen as well as adequate land for gardens and pastures and boreholes in villages; and Mr. Andrew Mponda, U.F.P. candidate for Blantyre Rural, mentioned raising the pay of chiefs and headmen.

Mr. Ross was the only candidate whose statement commented on the programme of his opponent. He remarked that the U.F.P. list of 'beliefs' did not mention the existence of nationalism, that it ignored the findings of the Monckton Commission and the imminence of a conference to review the federal constitution, and that it did not deal with the problems of peasant agriculture, which in his view could only be solved by 'harnessing the dynamic force of nationalism'. His plans for economic development were the same as those of the other Malawi-sponsored independents, but he asserted that they depended on 'the enthusiasm of the village people which can only be stimulated and maintained at this time through a feeling of confidence and participation in the government of the country'.

He rejected as 'disastrous' the U.F.P. proposal to create a unified federal civil service, pointing out that this would put an end to overseas recruitment. He referred to the neglect of secondary education by the

E

U.F.P. and asked where they were to get the teachers for the technical, domestic and primary education on which they proposed to concentrate.

He rejected the U.F.P. conception of multi-racial partnership on the ground that it 'entrenches racial groupings' and stood for 'a democratic society where, as soon as possible, everyone should be qualified to vote'.

5. THE CAMPAIGN

THE LOWER ROLL—MALAWI

During the registration period Malawi activity was concentrated entirely on securing the maximum number of registrations. Everyone qualified to register on the higher roll was urged to do so, apart from those who expected to be candidates in lower roll constituencies. The meeting on 21 January at which Dr. Banda launched the watchword 'Peace and Calm', and which so unfortunately ended in a breach of the peace, might perhaps be described as the opening of his campaign. At Chileka airport when leaving for a visit to the United Kingdom and United States in April he urged the crowd to disregard the C.L.P. as 'just an African branch of the U.F.P'. In London a few days later he said he was so confident of success that he would do no electioneering. However he proved in fact a tireless electioneer, speaking several times a week from the beginning of June right up to polling day.

His meetings drew crowds which relatively sober observers estimated at up to 10,000. Malawi supporters admitted that the much higher figures given in *Malawi News* were deliberately exaggerated, arguing that this was necessary to counter deliberate underestimation of the numbers by the police.

The procedure was more or less stereotyped. A striking characteristic to anyone accustomed to the British method of playing the election game was the insignificant part allotted to the candidate himself. At the final meeting at Ndirande outside Blantyre, the crowd arrived in taxis, buses and lorries as well as on foot. They were marshalled and kept in order by Malawi Youth contingents, some in red shirts embroidered with 'Malawi Freedom', others in tunic and trousers of military type; the latter were sometimes described as 'Dr. Banda's Special Branch'. Women's League members had a distinctive garb for every branch. Some of them lined the route by which the Doctor walked from his car to the platform, and the path was carpeted with women's cloths (the length of material by which a woman fastens a baby to her back). An efficient loudspeaker system was organized—in this case by a young electrician who had lost his job after being detained during the emergency. For an hour or so cheer leaders exchanged slogans with the crowd. Names of party leaders were called out, beginning with Kamuzu and proceeding in crescendo to Chipembere (fortissimo). The cheer leader then reminded the crowd of the Malawi colours and called out the names of all the candidates. Then 'atsamunda' (settlers) and the names of the 'stooges' who had allied themselves with the 'stupid federation' were answered with shouts of 'Zii'. At length, punctual, on this occasion, to the minute, the Doctor's 'motorcade' of seven cars appeared. A bugle played as he walked to the platform to an accompaniment of clapping, ululations and shouts of 'Kamuzu! Kwaca! [Dawn]'.

After an address of welcome he made a speech in English, which was interpreted into Cinyanja. This was largely concerned with his own leadership and achievements. He rebutted the assertions of the 'United Fools' Party' that his popularity was waning. Who would draw a larger crowd, he or the Governor? 'I came to break this stupid federation and to give you self-government in this country' (loud applause). 'People must fight for freedom; you don't get freedom by saying "Inde Bwana".' 'I said to Dixon, "This is not Northern Rhodesia, this is Nyasaland".' Dr. Banda then recapitulated at great length the events of the emergency and his release ('Did you even hear of Manoah [Wellington] Chirwa having a shave at Government House?'). 'On April 5 we heard we were to have a new constitution—and why continue a war when you have won?' 'No trouble to the white men, no trouble to the Indians, no trouble to the stooges either—they are dead dogs.' 'Do you think we could have got this constitution if I had agreed in 1959?' (a shrewd point). Dr. Banda said he had told the Secretary of State that he wanted no more nomination of Ministers. After speaking for an hour or more he concluded, 'Under the rules of Congress I alone decide who are to be candidates. I am here to give you your lower roll candidate. Stand up, Augustine!' The candidate came forward and was robed in a gown in the Malawi colours, red, green and black. He stood modestly silent while the Doctor presented him to the crowd as 'my representative. . . . Bwanausi represents Kamuzu'. Nothing was said about the candidate's qualities or achievements. Dr. Banda then explained the voting process and the significance of the Malawi symbol. He went on to say that after independence people would have to work harder than ever in order to raise the necessary revenues for social services. 'Does it mean,' he asked the audience, 'you do not want Europeans here?' (Shouts of 'No'.) 'I have nothing against Europeans. I did not come here to drive them away. What I hate is to have domination. To those who think they were created to rule I say, "Pack up and go now, *now*,

NOW!"' This statement was greeted with immense applause. In general, where European reporters were present, they gave publicity to it and not to the qualifying phrases which preceded it. Dr. Banda himself gave it more emphasis when speaking in the north, where anti-European feeling was strongest. After he reached this point in his Ndirande speech members of the audience began to get up and go away. However, the proceedings were not yet concluded, for he now publicly named Mrs. Rose Chibambo's latest baby, calling it Tanyada (We are proud) in celebration of independence.

At some meetings Dr. Banda invited any U.F.P. supporters to stand up, and when nobody responded, described them as 'cowards and hyenas who move at night'.

Constituency activity began as soon as the names of the candidates had been announced. Canvassing was the responsibility of the Malawi Youth. It consisted, not in soliciting promises to vote, but in drilling voters in polling procedures, in the name of the candidate and the party symbol. Senior party organizers approached Native Authorities and village headmen to engage their influence. They had most difficulty with those Native Authorities who had suffered violence during the disturbances. The village headmen, who have no powers of coercion, had been in a less invidious position in those days. Each was the senior man of a small kin group forming the nucleus of his village, so that his views carried whatever weight still attaches to seniority in contemporary Africa; in the rural areas doubtless a good deal. Although all headmen were entitled to vote, not all had registered.

The regulations requiring that permission be requested a fortnight in advance of any public meeting and that the names of the speakers be submitted were not modified, but they were administered with leniency. They created difficulties when, for example, branch officials failed to make the necessary preparations for a meeting and it proved impossible to get permission to change the date.

However, there was considerable activity in the form of 'committee meetings'. Permission was not required for meetings held in private places and not open to the public, and Malawi stretched this principle to cover gatherings at which the only restriction was that imposed by space. They were held in houses or in small grass-fenced enclosures in which perhaps 200 people sat on mats on the ground, while village headmen, branch officials and other notables were on chairs with the candidate in the centre. Many of those present were non-voters; on the other hand, probably all the voters present were members of the branch which had organized the meeting.

An example of such a meeting in a rural area was one held in Chiradzulu. The proceedings opened and closed with prayer. Then the candidate shouted Malawi slogans to which the audience responded. His discourse emphasized two themes as all-important—secession and independence; the case for secession was illustrated by examples of legislation in Southern Rhodesia. The composition of the new legislature was explained and the date of the election impressed on the audience; this was the day of passing from slavery to freedom, the day of the departure of Israel from Egypt, led by the saviour, the messiah, Dr. Banda, who had already rescued his people from the hated agricultural regulations.[1] The audience was reminded that Chiradzulu had been the home of freedom fighters from the time of John Chilembwe. Considerable time was spent in explaining the method of voting and the party symbol, and also the necessity of maintaining complete order on polling day. A presentation was made to the candidate of fowls, eggs, vegetables, chickens, and a goat. Songs were sung by the local Malawi Youth. One, emphasizing the position of the candidate as the chosen representative of the leader, linked his name with Dr. Banda's thus:

'Tidzasankha ndani? A Kamuzu Banda.
Tidzasankha ndani? A Chokani Banda.'

'Whom shall we choose? Kamuzu Banda.
Whom shall we choose? Chokani Banda.'

Mr. Bwanausi's addresses in the Blantyre Urban constituency gave more attention to matters of practical policy. Malawi would introduce universal education, and Malawi Youth would organize adult literacy classes. Kamuzu would get rid of unemployment, would bring work to Nyasaland; wages would be higher and rents lower; water supplies would be improved in rural areas.

A reasoned statement of the Malawi position, in addition to that in the manifesto, was given in the three recorded talks by D. Y. Chisiza which were broadcast from Dar-es-Salaam; each was repeated three times. They were also published in *Malawi News*.[2]

The first talk was an indictment of the United Federal Party under sixteen heads. It had sent federal troops to Nyasaland when the emergency was declared (this is remembered with extreme bitterness). It had 'prevented the British Government' from giving Africans parity representation in 1956. It had declared pro-Africans prohibited immigrants; stopped Nyasaland students going to India; 'sacked' employees

---

[1] Penalizing farmers for failure to obey soil conservation rules. Towards the end of 1960 Dr. Banda intervened on behalf of a number of people in the Southern Province who had been fined under these rules, and shortly afterwards it was announced that there would be no more prosecutions.

[2] 27 July 1961.

who refused to join the federal services; tried to get Dominion status without African consent; sent supplies to Tshombe; allowed Portuguese generals to visit Salisbury; and in addition introduced discriminatory laws and opposed attempts to remove discrimination. The second broadcast described Malawi's 'unsurpassable record'. It had 'secured an African majority in the teeth of European opposition'; restored African self-respect; put an end to an agricultural policy 'designed to victimize rather than educate the peasant'; 'fearlessly exposed the iniquitous policies of the colonial government'; and 'fought settler domination'. The third talk contrasted the leaders of the two parties and invited voters to choose between an ex-locomotive driver (Sir Roy Welensky) and an M.D. and B.Ph. [sic].

THE LOWER ROLL—THE U.F.P.

The U.F.P. concentrated their activities among lower roll voters on the Central Province, where they looked for support to village head-men and Master Farmers[1] who had been maltreated, or at least insulted as 'stooges', in the period of disturbances. They claimed large numbers of members; the totals may have been swollen by the reports of their African organizers. They did however sometimes hold branch meetings of three or four hundred Africans in Lilongwe.

They announced the opening of their campaign as far back as November 1960 with a meeting at Kota Kota. There was believed to be some hostility to Malawi in this district, based in part on tribal affiliations with the Nkata Bay supporters of T. D. T. Banda and in part on disappointment that resistance to authority had not produced quicker results. It was to counteract this feeling, it was said, that Malawi had chosen Kota Kota as the venue for the grand rally held after the release of the last detainees. In April meetings of chiefs in the Southern and Central Provinces were addressed, at their own request, according to press reports, by Mr. John Foot, a federal M.P., on the significance of federation.[2]

An appeal for election funds was launched early in April. 'Here is your opportunity,' the advertisement said, 'to show your support for the party which believes in law and order, prosperity for all peoples, and FREEDOM from oppression and intimidation.'[3]

Right up to nomination day U.F.P. organizers were maintaining that they could not hold public meetings for fear of molestation. Outside U.F.P. ranks the general opinion was that violence or threats of violence by Malawi supporters against their opponents had very much decreased since Dr. Banda's call for peace and calm, and in the middle

---

[1] See p. 11.   [2] Nyasaland Times, 14 April.   [3] Ibid., 21 April.

of May the *Nyasaland Forum*[1] reported that U.F.P. organizers were touring the country speaking and distributing literature and were not being molested. Of course it is likely that people who attended public meetings would have to face adverse comment from their friends. But the reliance of Malawi on 'intimidation' had become so central a theme of the U.F.P. campaign that it was hardly possible for them not to see this as a serious danger. What was interesting was to hear a defector from the U.F.P. deny that he had experienced any while engaged in propaganda for it. Of course such statements are not evidence; they merely show that this was an issue on which party orthodoxy on both sides had priority over individual experience. How far acts of violence were inspired or countenanced by Malawi leadership is another question again.

Thirty-six paid organizers were actually at work by the end of June, half of them in the Southern Province, and support for the party was said to be increasing at a greater rate than actual membership. Some organizers seem to have been rather too eager to enrol well-known African names, and letters indignantly repudiating membership appeared from time to time in the African press; according to the U.F.P. some of the writers were forced by threats to make these statements.

The molestation of newsvendors selling the party paper, *Timvane*, was sufficiently real for this mode of distribution to be given up. Ten thousand copies were printed, however, and distributed by post to members and to senior African civil servants, by hand and broadcast from landrovers in the villages. According to a Malawi sympathizer, those which were scattered broadcast were picked up and burnt. Only three numbers of this journal were published. It consisted of eight pages, at least a quarter of which were taken up by photographs, with reading matter in Cinyanja and English. The party initials were interpreted to mean 'Unity, Freedom, Partnership' or 'Umodzi Funani Pakumvana' [Together seek understanding]. A later version which appeared on the party lorries substituted 'Ufulu' [Freedom] for 'Umodzi'.

Two main lines of argument were presented—the benefits of federation and the iniquities of Malawi. Mr. Mathews Phiri wrote that his early fears of the consequences of federation had proved unfounded. An article explained that segregation was not in fact practised in the University College; a statement by the party chairman in Nyasaland assured readers that federal independence would not remove safeguards against racial discrimination. Specific arguments against federation current in Nyasaland were rebutted. Sir Roy Welensky's views on the importance of 'the moderate African' were summarized in the context

[1] 16 May.

of the Northern Rhodesia constitution. A curious article complained of the 'unseemly haste' with which the elections were being introduced while the public did not understand the process.

Sentences passed on persons accused of intimidation were reported. A letter described the case during the disturbances of a young woman who was not allowed to board a bus until she had bought a Malawi card, and suggested that all Malawi support was obtained in this way. A leader pointed out that Dr. Banda had not in fact achieved all that he claimed, and asked if he was 'somebody's stooge'. He was accused of taking shillings from little children; the party was invited to publish a balance sheet, and it was suggested that all the funds went in high living for the officials. Alleged dissensions within the party were mentioned. It was predicted that 'Malawi stooges' would stand as independents. Emphasis was laid on Dr. Banda's alleged promises that independence would make everybody rich. Two absurd abusive letters of the kind that semi-literate people often write were printed to show 'the kind of hatred that Malawi breeds'.

Photographs in the first issue showed party leaders, European and African, and prosperous Nyasalanders who were stated to have become so as the result of federation. In the other two issues they merely illustrated topicalities.

In appealing to a wider audience the U.F.P. made use of advertisements in the press, and also, in the week before polling day, had leaflets dropped from an aeroplane; these last attracted very little attention.

The Christian Liberation Party opened its campaign in mid-April with a meeting at Fort Johnston, the theme being 'We are up to liberate all from all forms of intimidation, violence and similar vicious practices'.[1] At Nkata Bay its secretary-general, Mr. Pondeponde, accused Malawi of being unchristian because they had once had a church service cancelled at a time fixed for a party meeting. Meantime Mr. Katsonga was touring the Port Herald District with a band singing anti-Malawi songs, and Mr. T. D. T. Banda was touring the north. At Cholo on 7 May Mr. Katsonga warned an audience of 200 that Malawi was creating a 'Congo situation' in Nyasaland. Mr. Kwenje said the C.L.P. differed from Malawi only in their attitude towards intimidation, and another party official said Malawi was 'still living in the days of Lobengula'.

As the time of the election came nearer, however, it became obvious that it was futile for any organization other than Malawi to try to draw Africans to public meetings. People who did not support Malawi simply did not like to declare this publicly. When a meeting was announced in Blantyre anyone who appeared to be going to it might be asked what

[1] *Nyasaland Forum*, 18 April.

he was up to by friends who met him, or called names before or after. According to the U.F.P. they were threatened with dire fates including death by witchcraft. But if the hostility of Africans to those whom they regard as collaborating with the enemy is expressed in threats which Europeans would not employ, it is not different in essence from what racialist Europeans show towards 'white Kaffirs', nor did it make these elections, as Mr. Blackwood asserted, completely different from what is understood by the word in the United Kingdom.

On nomination day Dr. Banda and the Malawi candidates for four of the five lower roll seats in the Northern Province were returned unopposed. The young man who had been put up to oppose Dr. Banda could not get the required signatures for his nomination; it appeared later that he was not in any case a registered voter. The wife of a Malawi Youth member set fire to his house, as she had several times threatened to do. She was sentenced to three months' imprisonment.

The Federal Broadcasting Corporation offered time on the air to all organized parties. Malawi refused the offer on the ground that the Corporation was an instrument of federal propaganda, and made their own arrangements with the Tanganyika broadcasting service. The independents asked the F.B.C. to give them time as a group, possibly for a joint appearance of the 'brains trust' type, but were told that it would be contrary to the principles followed by the B.B.C. to give broadcasting time to independents.

Lower roll candidates of the U.F.P. and C.L.P. operated through personal contacts. They sought the support of chiefs and village headmen and of the circle of friends on which each could count. But even with the restricted Nyasaland franchise there were too many voters for anyone's personal following to sway the result.

In the week before polling day the U.F.P. published in the *Nyasaland Forum*[1] a full page advertisement impressing on readers the secrecy of the vote and giving a Cinyanja translation of the party manifesto. In the same issue Mr. Kwenje (C.L.P.) published a statement that he had always opposed federation and had appeared before the Monckton Commission in order to do so. Otherwise the propaganda of the C.L.P. consisted largely in letters by its secretary to this newspaper.

THE HIGHER ROLL

Direct controversy was confined to the higher roll, though here it was conducted for the most part at long range. Two independents, Mr. Cameron and Mr. Ross, invited their opponents to meet them in debate but were refused. Mr. Roopsingh, however, took a full page in the *Nyasaland Times*[2] to explain that he wanted nearly everything that Mr.

[1] 8 August.   [2] 11 August.

Cameron wanted, but held that these aims could only be attained through the maintenance of the federation. He rejected the policy of building roads by manual labour, but this was not an issue that aroused any interest.

Mr. Cameron, greatly daring, challenged Sir Roy Welensky to debate with him during his tour of Nyasaland in the first week of August, but was told that the Prime Minister's time was fully committed. He also held a private meeting for his European constituents at which he was prepared to deal with their objections to his policy, but only his friends turned up.

Although the Malawi manifesto did not mention the subject of federation, nobody doubted that the election was, as *Malawi News*[1] put it on the eve of the poll, a referendum on this question. Lower roll voters were given the impression by Malawi that the 'stupid federation' was already dead and would be formally buried on polling day; and by the C.L.P. that the determination of Malawi to bury it was not single-minded enough.

In the higher roll contests the U.F.P. argued the advantages of federation, while their opponents maintained that the existing federation was operated in the interests of Salisbury, that the U.F.P. was directed from Salisbury, and that its promise of partnership had not been implemented during the eight years of federation and was in any case not a sound basis for race relations. The U.F.P. did not deal with the last point except by appropriating the adjective 'non-racial'.

The central argument for the maintenance of federation was the economic one. As the campaign went on this came to be put in the form of a question to the independents, 'Where's the money coming from?' U.F.P. candidates emphasized the shaky financial position of Nyasaland, its limited resources and the unlikelihood of its securing external aid except as a member of the federation. The independents replied that it was clearly desirable for Nyasaland to be linked with its neighbours but these links must be freely chosen. Most of them gave little attention to the sources of capital for the developments they advocated; they agreed with the U.F.P. that political stability was necessary to attract foreign investment, but did not believe that this could be attained within the framework of the existing federation. One independent asserted that funds had already been promised from foreign sources; another said that in view of the vast sums which the United Kingdom was spending on armaments it could obviously afford the relatively small amount required by Nyasaland.

The U.F.P., however, placed more reliance on other arguments. They quoted statements by British politicians favouring the maintenance

[1] 14 August.

of federation, and reproduced these a week before polling day in a full-page advertisement in the *Nyasaland Times*.[1] From the words of Mr. Lennox-Boyd that 'it is the duty of every loyal person in the Territory to lend all his efforts to making the Federation a success' Mr. Blackwood drew the argument that it was treasonable to propose secession, and this was the keynote of his eve-of-the-poll broadcast, published as an advertisement in the *Nyasaland Times*.[2] Only one independent thought of quoting the Monckton Commission in a manifesto and one in a speech.

The U.F.P. opened their campaign with the assertion that federation 'can, must and shall' be maintained. But they were in a delicate position in that there was really no chance of their securing a majority of the seats in the legislature. At one time this was in fact mentioned as a possibility; at another Mr. Blackwood said 'the government' would secure a majority for 'its' policy by nomination (on the assumption that the civil service Ministers would continue to control policy and would insist on the maintenance of federation?). On other occasions speakers urged the importance of winning enough higher roll seats to be sure of two Ministries. There was some doubt how many these would be; Mr. Little said the party would need all eight. When speakers accepted the certainty that they would be in the minority in the legislature they urged the need for a 'balanced executive' in which the U.F.P. would temper the extremism of Malawi; it was not clear what function this argument allotted to the civil service Ministers.

As the main opposition on the higher roll came from independents, the U.F.P. attacked the independent position as such. Since the independents had expressly rejected the idea of forming a bloc, it was fair to say, as Mr. Blackwood did, that they were 'united only by their antipathies'; and since their antipathy was to the U.F.P., it was fair to argue that a vote for them was tantamount to a vote for Malawi (though not so fair to call it a vote for 'a rural slum and a bankrupt dictatorship'). At the first U.F.P. meeting Mr. Roopsingh made the curious statement that independents with the endorsement of a party were found only in Communist countries, but this line of argument was not pursued. The U.F.P. sought to show that the constitution allowed no place for independents. They could not be Ministers because they did not represent anyone; because they could not 'take the government whip' or 'impose the government whip' on anyone else (a dear old lady asked what was meant by 'taking the whip'); because the constitution said the Governor was to appoint Ministers after consulting the leaders of parties and did not mention independents. Mr. Little circulated the clause in question in a letter to his constituents.

[1] 8 August.   [2] 15 August.

Mr. Blackwood's positive policy was built round the slogan 'security'. His promises included security of person and property by the provision of adequate police and federal forces; security from further constitutional changes 'before progress has been achieved'; security from intimidation (he was prepared to make boycotts illegal); and security from Colonial Office interference by the creation of a Council of State. His opponents did not discuss any of these points. He defended himself against the charge of hostility towards the civil service by disclaiming responsibility for the 'Blackwood boxes',[1] and against that of subservience to the interests of Southern Rhodesia by recalling that he was wont to protest against aspects of the federal tax system which were unfair to Nyasaland.

In all but one of the higher roll constituencies European voters were in a large majority, and U.F.P. arguments were addressed to them only, though their opponents sought to appeal to the Asian community. In Soche, however, the outcome depended upon the Asian vote. The U.F.P. candidate recognized this to the extent of referring to the provision made from federal funds for Asian education. At the opening meeting, where three candidates and a federal M.P. were together on the platform, the whole team were nonplussed by a question from the floor about immigration policy, but finally someone conceded that the immigration of Asian doctors might be permitted. This was a difficult question also for Mr. Cameron, who would not concede that immigration should not be controlled in African interests. He did however advocate the admission of more Asians to the civil service.

The appeal to the Asian voters was mainly organized by Mr. Sacranie, whose energy in campaigning was second only to that of the Doctor himself. He organized two meetings for Asians at which Dr. Banda repeated his promises of friendship towards them. At each of these he spoke himself at some length. He made a great point of the argument that Dr. Banda had secured the recognition of Gujerati as 'an official language' (i.e. by having literacy in Gujerati recognized as a qualification for the franchise). He reminded Asians of the disabilities that they suffered under current federal policies, and also of derogatory remarks made about their community by Mr. Blackwood. In particular he quoted the latter's comments on Indian marriage at the time when women 'married under any system which permits polygamy' were denied the federal vote. He also hinted at the unfortunate consequences for Afro-Asian co-operation that might follow from the election of a U.F.P. candidate by a predominantly Asian vote.

A question which gave rise to some feeling at the height of the campaign was the terms of service of expatriate civil servants. In October

[1] Very small houses built for civil servants.

1960 the United Kingdom government had issued a white paper offering to contribute from its own revenues that part of a revised scale of payments which was classified as 'inducement allowances'. The details of the new salary scales were to be agreed in discussion with the different territorial governments, and a Nyasaland delegation was in London for this purpose in July 1961. When the first reports of their talks appeared in the press, it seemed that the increases agreed on were less than what had been confidently expected, and this was ascribed to intervention by Sir Roy Welensky. The U.F.P., while indignantly repudiating the charge of hostility towards expatriate civil servants, pointed to the financial burden of raising the pay of locally recruited men to the level proposed for expatriates.

The party did, in fact, depend on intervention by Sir Roy in the sense that he lent them his support in a three-day speaking tour. This was described in advance as a 'barnstorming tour', but in fact it consisted in three or four private meetings. The Prime Minister, it was explained, must not be exposed to humiliating incidents. His audiences, therefore, were loyal U.F.P. members rather than floating voters. His speeches doubtless had their effect in securing a high poll of convinced federationists.

INTIMIDATION

A few days before his arrival, nine houses were burnt down in a small area in the Kota Kota district. One was the home of a Malawi supporter; four were houses of Master Farmers who supported the U.F.P. The stormy petrel Mr. Makamo[1] was in one of these houses. Police stated that the burnings were not inspired by political motives. Dr. Banda issued a statement in *Malawi News*[2] condemning all such breaches of the peace, and reiterating his orders to his followers that peace and calm should be maintained 'before, during and after the elections'.

Mr. Blackwood, however, took this incident as evidence of a general state of lawlessness in the country, and proposed that the elections be postponed for two or three months while order was restored. Mr. Sawyer, the candidate for Lilongwe District, went one better and suggested that a delay of eighteen months to two years was called for. He asserted that Asians and Africans who attended U.F.P. meetings were trembling with fear, and that he could think of nothing like it since Hitler's Germany. Mr. Sawyer was actually too young to have had much experience of Hitler's Germany; a few other people, however, recalled one of the more sinister incidents in the rise of Hitlerism.[3]

[1] *See* p. 49.
[2] 31 July.
[3] After the election a number of U.F.P. supporters who had accused Malawi

Even the *Nyasaland Times*[1] did not support the U.F.P. on this occasion. In their view only an insurrection could justify postponement, and nothing was more likely than postponement to provoke an insurrection.

The party appealed to Sir Roy Welensky to use his influence with the British government. He reacted with a skilfully tempered mixture of bluster and caution. According to a statement broadcast on the morning of 2 August, he said that after examining the situation for himself he would decide whether or not to ask Mr. Macmillan to postpone the elections. When he arrived in Nyasaland he announced that he 'would let the British Prime Minister know the exact depth of his feelings',[2] but did not mention postponement. On leaving he said he would consult with his colleagues and decide what to do. On the last night of his visit a broadcast statement by the Governor, who had also been touring the country, that conditions everywhere were peaceful, was followed immediately by one from Sir Roy to the effect that any denial of the extent of intimidation was 'idle talk'.

Meantime the Rhodesia lobby at Westminster had been active. A question had been asked about the desirability of postponing the election, and Mr. Callaghan had been sufficiently perturbed to send a telegram to Dr. Banda asking for reassurance. The Colonial Secretary, however, had stated that he had full confidence in the judgment of the Governor and saw no reason for postponement.

But there were more variations on the theme of intimidation to come. On the night of 6 August an Indian store-owner was murdered in Blantyre. He was gagged and bound, and the police supposed that his assailants had intended to rob but not kill him. But as he had not been robbed, no motive for the murder was apparent. The crime was unlike any of which Malawi supporters had ever been accused. Nevertheless, the report circulated that it was an act of reprisal because the old man had attended a gathering to meet Sir Roy. As he was not on the higher roll, this was unlikely; nor did the dozen or so Indians who are known to have been there come to any harm. Mr. Roopsingh went to the funeral, and Mr. Cameron's supporters began to wonder if the incident would lead many Asians to seek the protection of the U.F.P., or, what might have been just as serious for him, stay at home on polling day. *Malawi News*[3] stated that 'Mr. Kakubhai's death has caused great

Youth members of burning houses were charged with making wrongful accusations and convicted, and were required to pay compensation to Malawi members who had been wrongfully imprisoned. Some were also convicted of setting fire to their own houses.

[1] 4 August.
[2] *Rhodesia Herald*, 4 August.
[3] 7 August.

shock for he was a fond friend of the people of Malawi', and a statement issued by the Asian Convention condemned the 'disgraceful tactic of trying to treat his death as political capital'.[1]

The other source of reports of intimidation was Nkata Bay, whence came complaints from Mr. T. D. T. Banda several times a week. Reports from impartial observers were that he was not prevented from holding meetings but was sometimes severely heckled. Mr. Orton Chirwa's clerk agreed that Mr. Banda had difficulty in travelling in the daytime, not, he said, because he was attacked but because young boys would stand across the road and politely ask him not to go that way. On the morning of polling day he telegraphed the Supervisor of Elections that he was withdrawing his candidature because of intimidation.

POLLING DAY

There was no doubt about the determination of Malawi headquarters that the polling should be quiet and orderly. Instructions went out to all candidates that Malawi Youth bands were not to be in evidence, that women were not to appear dressed in the party colours, that people should 'even forget their Banda badges'. In fact the voting had almost the solemnity of a religious ritual. No police control was necessary. Most of the voters assembled at the polling stations an hour or more before the opening time (6.30 a.m.) and formed into silent queues. At one station in the Central Province 400 voters arrived the night before and camped out. At another, women voters were allowed to go through first. People from the same village kept together (whether or not because they had come in a body) and this made the checking of names easy. Very few voters had lost their means of identification—registration slips or tax receipts. One or two hopefully offered rejection slips as evidence of their right to vote, but made no trouble when they were turned away. A very small number failed to put their ballot papers into the boxes. Nobody spent a long time in the polling booth pondering his choice, as is said to have happened elsewhere. Indeed in the Central Province voters passed through at the rate of 200 an hour. One or two people are said to have put tax receipts into the ballot box as well as their voting papers. At the rural stations the queues had disappeared by 9.30 or 10 a.m., and in some cases all those registered except about a dozen had actually voted by that time.

Polling agents of the opposition parties were seldom to be seen; it was not surprising if nobody wished to expose himself to the almost unanimously hostile gaze of a long procession of his neighbours. I saw

[1] *Malawi News*, 10 August.

one U.F.P. candidate, Mr. Kumbikano, at a polling station sitting with the Malawi agent, but he said he was only waiting for his wife to vote. It is doubtful whether most of the Malawi polling agents understood what their functions were. I only saw one who had a copy of the voters' register and was marking names—a young woman secretary from the party headquarters.

The victory of Malawi in all twenty lower roll constituencies did not surprise anyone, but not everyone expected the very high poll and the very small number of votes for opposition candidates. As Malawi had prophesied from the first, every one of these lost his deposit. Only Mr. Chinyama, in Lilongwe South, got over a hundred votes; Mr. T. D. T. Banda got only twelve. The poll was over 90 per cent in every constituency.

The poll in the higher roll constituencies was less spectacular, but would have been regarded as satisfactory in a European election. The lowest percentage was 75, in both the Northern Province and Lilongwe Districts, the highest 91 in Limbe. In all the others the poll was over 80 per cent. No deposits were lost.

The U.F.P. won five seats—Blantyre (Mr. Blackburn), Limbe (Mr. Little), Southern Districts (Mr. Peterkins), Lilongwe Town (Mr. Morgan) and Shire North (Mr. Duncan). Thus the three sitting members were returned, and whatever may have been the dissatisfaction of European voters with the U.F.P. or with their individual record, it was not enough to cause a significant swing away from them. In Blantyre it was calculated that only twenty-five Europeans could have voted for the independent candidate; in Limbe the 152 votes cast against Mr. Little were less than the total of 184 non-European voters, and the same was true of the 121 votes against Mr. Peterkins in the Southern Districts and the 107 against Mr. Morgan in Lilongwe Town.

The one U.F.P. victory to cause surprise was that in the three-cornered contest in Shire North. It had been assumed that the U.F.P. could count only on the forty or fifty farmers in the constituency and that the civil servants were on the whole opposed to it, and speculation had turned on the relative prospects of the two independents. In the event these polled 150 votes each while Mr. Duncan received 210. It is impossible to judge whether, if Mr. Mtawali had not stood, all his votes would have gone to Major Moxon. If there were more than 90 voters who believed with the U.F.P. that divorce should be a disqualification for political activity,[1] and so would have abstained rather than vote for a divorced husband (and there were certainly some), then Mr. Duncan would have won in any case. In this constituency votes were not divided on racial lines. As there were only 130 non-European

[1] See p. 14.

voters, a number of European votes must have gone to each of the independents.

Mr. Cameron in Soche won 398 votes, a majority of 109 over Mr. Roopsingh; he could have secured this total without any votes from Europeans.

The two Malawi higher roll candidates who were successful, however, must have won the support of European voters, at least 36 in the case of Mr. Surtee and at least 38 in the case of Mr. Mkandawire. These were the two constituencies where the poll was lowest. In the Northern Province, with 203 European voters registered, only 73 voted U.F.P.

Speculation was rife before and after the election about the basis on which the elected Ministers would be chosen. The view of the U.F.P. was that their majority of seats on the higher roll entitled them to both higher roll ministries, and Mr. Blackwood would not accept anything less. Dr. Banda, for his part, objected to the idea of a coalition ministry.

Eventually the Executive Council was made up without any U.F.P. members, as would have been expected by most students of the theory of cabinet government. The Ministers elected on the lower roll were Dr. Banda (Natural Resources and Local Government); Mr. Chiume (Education); and Mr. Bwanausi (Labour). The party's legal and economic experts became parliamentary secretaries, Mr. Chirwa to the Ministry of Justice and Mr. Chisiza to the Ministry of Finance. From the higher roll Mr. Cameron, the successful independent, was appointed Minister of Works and Transport, and Mr. Mkandawire Minister without Portfolio.

6. CONCLUSIONS

THESE elections do not provide much material for illuminating generalizations. The lower roll results cannot be interpreted in terms of local differences, since experience was everywhere the same. A general interpretation of the African attitude would seem to be that the election provided, not an opportunity to test the support for alternative views, but an occasion for a demonstration of solidarity, a comment that might also be made on the African referendum on the Southern Rhodesia constitution held a few weeks earlier. The very high poll is certainly to be explained in this way rather than by any doubt as to the outcome. It appears also that a high poll at the first elections ever held has been common in Africa, and is explained by the novelty of the event, by a general vague belief that it heralds the dawning of a new day, and by the intensive propaganda directed at voters, much of which is

F

omitted on later occasions. It was clear to voters that they were choosing men to replace those at present playing an important part in government. Perhaps it was not quite so clear what part would be theirs 'when we go to Zomba'; but is this clear to many voters in western Europe?

Studies of this kind often mention the quaint views expressed by African voters about the meaning of what they are doing. No less quaint in Nyasaland were some of the views heard during the canvassing of Europeans, which showed very clearly that people who have spent their adult life in a country without representative government do not understand the significance of the electoral process even if it is a part of their country's tradition, and even if they have had eleven years' compulsory education. This unfamiliarity in part explains the shocked horror with which the U.F.P. contrasted the pressures operating on African voters with an imaginary ideal election in which every vote is cast as a result of a wholly independent intellectual judgment of the merits of parties and candidates.

Some higher roll voters could not be induced to consider what candidate they should support, but simply inveighed against 'politics' as a discreditable activity and an interruption of serious work. Some could be brought to recognize that Dr. Banda was bound to have a majority in the new legislature, but could not understand what relation this had to their choice of candidate. Others were unaware that the new constitution had made any change in the balance of power, and assumed that by supporting the U.F.P. they could maintain the position which in fact had already been lost. One who went so far as to admit that Dr. Banda was bound to become a Minister commented that he would 'have to learn to co-operate'.

The maintenance of a dual roll, and indeed of a restricted franchise, is not likely to be practicable for long in Nyasaland, if experience elsewhere is to be taken as a guide. The attitude of higher roll voters does not always support the view that they are capable of exercising more responsible judgment in political matters than their fellow citizens, except in the restricted sense of the word 'responsible' to mean 'conservative'.

APPENDIX I

The Constitution of the Malawi Congress Party (M.C.P.)

I. NAME

The name of the Organization shall be 'THE MALAWI CONGRESS PARTY' (hereinafter called 'The Party').

II. AIMS AND OBJECTS

(a) To work relentlessly to achieve self-government and ultimate independence for the people of Nyasaland and their chiefs.

(b) To serve as the vigorous conscious political vanguard for removing all forms of oppression, racial, economic, social and otherwise, and for the establishment of a democratic government in Nyasaland.

(c) To secure and at all time maintain the unity of all the people and chiefs of Nyasaland.

(d) To work with and in the interest of the Trade Union Movement, and other kindred organizations, whose aims and objects are in harmony with this Constitution.

(e) To work for a speedy reconstruction of a better Nyasaland in which the people and their chiefs shall have the right to live and govern themselves.

(f) To promote the political, social and economic emancipation of the people, especially those who depend on their own exertions by hand or by brain for the means of life.

(g) To work with other nationalist democratic and socialist movements in Africa and other continents with a view to promoting Pan-Africanism.

III. MEMBERSHIP

There shall be two classes of Members, namely:

(i) Individual Members.
(ii) Affiliated Organizations.

INDIVIDUAL MEMBERS: Individual members shall be persons of not less than sixteen years of age who

(a) accept and conform to the Constitution, principles, programme and policy of the Party and its rules, and

(b) are not members of a political party or organization ancillary or subsidiary thereto or declared by the Annual Delegates Conference or National Committee in pursuance of Conference decisions to be ineligible for affiliations to the Party.

N.B. A Person shall be deemed to be a member of the Party when he shall have paid an entrance fee of *two* shillings and an annual subscription of *two* shillings.

AFFILIATED MEMBERS:
(a) Each affiliated organization must accept the programme, principles and policy of the Party, and
(b) agree to conform to the Constitution and Standing Orders of the Party and its rules.
(c) Affiliated organizations shall pay an affiliation fee of *two pounds* a year.
(d) The Party shall not enter into affiliation with or give support financially or otherwise to any political party or organization proscribed by the Annual Delegates Conference.

IV. METHOD OF MANAGEMENT

There shall be established in every district and province branches district and provincial Parties.

(i) Every Branch shall have at least ten members.
(ii) Every District Party, consisting of all branches in the district shall have the District Chairman as its leader and shall meet once a month.
(iii) The Provincial Party shall meet quarterly and its leader shall be elected once every year and the candidates shall be subject to the approval of the Central Executive Committee.

V. MANAGEMENT

1. The management of the Party shall be in the hands of the Central Executive Committee consisting of:

(i) *The President:* elected at an annual General Conference once every three years. The retiring President shall be eligible for re-election.
(ii) Such administrative Officers as shall be appointed by the President of the Party from among 10 names elected by the Provincial Committees to the Central Executive Committee and from among ten names elected by the Annual Delegates Conference to the Central Executive Committee.

N.B. The President in Committee shall have powers of dismissing officers and members of the Party.

2. *National Committee:* The National Committee shall consist of representatives one from each district elected by the District Party conference but the candidates for such election shall be approved by the Central Executive Committee.

The National Committee shall meet half-yearly to:
(a) receive and consider the report of the Central Executive Committee on the implementation of the policy of the Party as formulated and approved by the Annual Delegates Conference.
(b) prepare the agenda for the Annual Delegates Conference.

3. ANNUAL DELEGATES CONFERENCE: The Annual Delegates Conference shall be the highest authority of the Party and shall consist of Delegates appointed by the Branches. Every Delegate to the Conference must:

(a) individually accept and conform to the Constitution, programme, and policy of the Party and its rules;

(b) be a bona fide member or paid permanent official of the Party;
(c) not act as a delegate for more than one branch or organization.

The following shall not be eligible to act as delegates;

(a) persons who are members of political parties or organizations, ancillary or subsidiary thereto, declared by the Annual Conference of the Party or the National Committee in pursuance of the Conference decisions to be ineligible for affiliation to the Party.

(b) persons acting as candidates in opposition to duly endorsed Party Candidates.

N.B. An Emergency Delegates Conference may be held whenever the Central Executive Committee deems it necessary provided that two week's notice is given.

VI. DISCIPLINE

The Supreme Executive power of the Party shall be vested in the PRESIDENT as advised by the Central Executive Committee.

VII. FINANCE

1. The general funds of the Party shall be derived from proceeds of functions (such as dances) voluntary subscriptions, appeals, donations, bequests, sale of literature, badges, admission fees of members, membership fees and other sources approved by the Party.

2. There shall be a Standing Finance Committee consisting of six members elected at an Annual Delegates Conference which shall have powers of control over expenditure and shall assist in the raising of funds.

3. All the cheques above the sum of ten pounds (£10) shall not be made except with the permission of the Standing Finance Committee.

4. All the cheques shall bear the signature of the President and General Treasurer. In the case of the absence of the General Treasurer, the Secretary shall countersign all cheques.

5. No Bank overdraft shall be made without the approval of the President.

6. Any man collecting money for or on behalf of the Party shall immediately report to the Central Executive Committee. All money collected by branches or provincial Executives shall be sent to the Central Executive Committee which shall provide them with all their material and financial requirements.

7. All monies collected on behalf of the Party shall be receipted for and every receipt issued shall be fully accounted for. Receipt books shall be issued to branches and Provincial Executives free of charge, and all receipts stubs shall be immediately returned to the Central Executive Committee.

8. Regular receipts and receipt books shall be submitted by branches and provincial executives to the Central Executive Committee.

9. Branch and Provincial Executives collection and custody of money shall be made by the collector and Provincial Treasurer respectively.

VIII. YOUTH AND WOMEN'S ORGANIZATIONS

WOMEN and YOUTH shall be organized into the Party's Women's League and the Party Youth League respectively by the Executive Committee.

IX. GENERAL

1. No circulars shall be issued by Provincial, District or Branch Executives except with the permission or prior knowledge of the Central Executive Committee.

2. All letters to the press concerning the policy or activities of the Party shall be submitted to the Central Executive Committee for approval and despatch.

. Alterations to the Constitution shall be effected after a majority vote at an Annual Delegates Conference. Notices for such alterations shall be sent to the Central Executive Committee two months before the date of the Annual Conference.

APPENDIX II

Constitution of a Legal Organization Named:
Christian Democratic Party (C.D.P.)

1. The aim of the 'Christian Democratic Party' shall be to assure to all inhabitants 'Freedom and well being in a self-ruling and peaceful Nyasaland'.

2. This aim shall be pursued by all its members only through lawful and just means, recognizing all natural human rights and adhering to Christian principles.

3. The Christian Democratic Party claims for all inhabitants of Nyasaland, as equal citizens, the same individual and social rights and duties.

4. The C.D.P. wants the people of Nyasaland to be free from all sorts of oppression, discrimination and intimidation and to enjoy well being and peace under truly Democratic Government.

5. The C.D.P. will, subject only to good order and morality in particular, assure to everybody freedom and the rights:

    (a) to think, speak and write according to one's personal conviction.
    (b) to believe, worship, act and live to one's religious creed.
    (c) to possess property, individual or in partnership according to law and justice.

6. The C.D.P. will work for the well being of all by promoting more individual social and economic development:

    (a) individual development by obtaining more facilities for higher education and technical training.
    (b) social development advocating friendly co-existence and fraternal co-operation with all, irrespective of colour, race or creed, basing promotion and remuneration only on ability and merit.
    (c) economic development to be obtained through:
    Better agricultural methods and better produce.
    More and bigger industries.
    Intensification of trade and commerce, higher skilled labour, harder work, and higher wages.

7. The C.D.P. assures peace to every inhabitant of good will in Nyasaland by way of justice and charity.